Backpacking Wisdom Of 50 Years

Timeless Guidance From Hard Knocks in the Wild

Mark Diehl

ISBN 979-8-9874044-0-9 (paperback) English

First edition December 2022

Printed in the United States of America

All cover and content photos are property of the author

Contact the author: 50yearsbackpacking@gmail.com

~~~

Dedicated to the unsung

heroes who build and

maintain our trails

~ ~ ~

Table of Contents

WHAT'S INSIDE ?

➢ Intended audience: beginner to intermediate

➢ Clear and concise guidance on selecting and using the essential and optional gear, and the methods for ensuring safe and comfortable adventures. What works ... and what doesn't work for:

- First Aid, Hygiene and Safety
- Hiking
- Fire and Water
- Shelter and Sleeping
- Footwear and Clothing
- Food and Cooking
- Gear Maintenance and Repair

➢ Five major sections are organized by a trip's key chronological activities: *Plan > Pack > Hike > Camp > Return/Unpack/Maintain*

➢ Covers winter camping, backpacking with children and maintaining your gear

➤ Appendices containing critical First-Aid procedures (in flashcard-ready format), essential knot tying and a nature treasure hunt for kids

➤ Checklists for assembling your backpack's contents and stocking a solid First-Aid kit

➤ Please note that this book is not intended to cover bug-out, *Shit Hits The Fan* (SHTF) conditions. There are countless excellent "prepper" books and web-based resources covering this topic, and the skills taught within them are worth visiting as some have potential applicability to backpacking.

INTRODUCTION

The guidance offered herein is my own, based on fifty years of experience in the field. All recommended gear was curated carefully and is readily available. I pack every recommended item, save for those noted as luxury items, which are optional and are to be chosen at your discretion.

Ounces truly do matter in this undertaking. A good rule of thumb is that your loaded pack weight (including the pack itself) should not exceed 20% of your body weight. That puts someone weighing 150 pounds at a 30 pound target pack weight, and a 200 pounder's target at 40 pounds. Use this as a general gauge to help determine which of the *Luxury Items* might be piled on. There are some such items that I'm packing every time, no matter the pack weight. For example, the camp chair ... I simply wouldn't leave home without it, given the comfort afforded.

I receive zero benefit from any product recommendations herein, nor do I receive any benefit from recommending that you foremost support your local gear purveyor, and also join a co-op such as REI who offers harder-to-find items.

Once you're geared up for backpacking, it is appreciably less expensive than many other leisure activities (not that we do it for the savings). Buy the best gear that you can afford and you'll be rewarded with years of low overhead enjoyment.

If you're new to backpacking and aren't quite sure if it's your bag, then don't invest initially in high-quality, expensive gear. Except for footwear, consider instead borrowing or renting the major gear (tent and backpack), if an option. You'll quickly learn what gear works best for you. If you develop into a lover of backpacking, you'll have plenty of opportunities to become a gear junky and, aside from the many rewards of actual backpacking, gear mongering is one of its main other enjoyments.

But before we jump into the nuts and bolts of backpacking, let's ponder for a moment … why go backpacking?

Consider the following rewards:

MIND

- Provides keen sense of adventure and accomplishment
- Improves the powers of observation
- Affords opportunity for deep thought / introspection
- Teaches self sufficiency and team building skills
- Promotes relationship bonding / camaraderie
- Sharpens sense of purpose / self

BODY

- Improves cardiovascular health
- Heightens sensory awareness
- Washes away the stresses of modernity

SPIRIT / SOUL

- Purity of nature recharges the soul
- Trips afford a pronounced "cleansed" feeling
- Connection to the land feeds our primal spirit
- Deepens relationship with mother earth

1. PLAN

As with any undertaking, a well-laid plan makes for better endeavors. This holds especially true for backpacking, where your health, safety, sustenance and comfort is entirely in your hands (on your back, as it were). Good planning was never so important.

Choose your destination and route first, then make planning decisions and adjustments based on terrain difficulty, trip length, altitude, campsite exposure, weather forecast, water and camp fire availability (each of these latter two important aspects will be addressed in detail). Figure on covering 1.5 miles per hour on a trail having minimal elevation gain/loss.

Study and carry a physical map of the route/area, ideally waterproof and the 7.5 minute topographical contour type (orderable at usgs.gov). Optionally, download map(s) to a phone-based app or use a stand-alone GPS mapping device.

Divide and conquer. Divvy up the load so that weight is equitably shared and duplicate items are avoided. For example, only one First-Aid kit and water purifier is typically needed.

Before departing:

Share your plan/route/map with trusted friends or family members who will be staying behind, and will call out the dogs should you not return when expected.

Obtain any permits that may be required (entrance / camping / camp fire, etc.)

Reserve food storage canister (bear protection) if applicable or mandatory.

Fully charge electronic devices, and battery backup, if applicable.

Clean your H2O filter.

Determine if anyone has a medical condition (including allergies). Be prepared by learning their care and treatment needs, including any meds involved.

Trim your toenails.

The Big Three ...

Nothing is more important than maintaining your **Health, Hygiene and Safety** on a backpacking trip. Throw any of these out of balance and your trip takes on a whole different dimension. Each will be reviewed in detail.

In addition to your party's collective responsibility for maintaining its well-being, there are other important aspects that can improve the odds. Here are a few:

- *Do not rush* to make up hiking time. Allow for ample slack time when route planning.
- *Consider any weak links* in your group. Does someone have an ailment that requires slowing the hiking pace, or re-distributing some of their weight load to others to ease their burden?
- *Do not tempt inclement weather*. Make camp BEFORE an impending storm unleashes.

- *Avoid setting up camp in the dark*

- *Don't be seduced by "mission zeal".* Use sound judgment and make camp sooner than planned if needed, or outright turn back if necessary.

i.   HEALTH (FIRST-AID)

Assemble a First-Aid kit using the checklist in *Appendix A*.

Understand the conditions that your First-Aid kit can and cannot handle. Learn its purposes, usage methods and limitations. For example, while this kit covers basic emergency preparedness, it is nowhere near what an EMT's kit contains.

My logic has always been that a First-Aid kit's robustness should increase as your planned trip's distance from help/rescue increases. A week-long wilderness backcountry trip warrants a more serious approach to First-Aid preparedness. I recommend studying wilderness First-Aid accordingly.

Foremost, understand the symptoms and treatment of the #1 hiker fatality cause: hypothermia (covered in *Appendix B*).

Let common sense be your guide, and always consider yourself as the last line of survival defense. As is taught for handling a firearm, the safety is between your ears.

Study *Appendix B - First-Aid Procedures*

Print and laminate *Appendix B* per its instructions. Store these flashcards in your First-Aid kit (your foolproof copy).

Tip: Photograph appendices *A* and *B* using your cell phone (that's right, as a backup to hardcopy).

Encourage others to study the flashcards. Conduct quizzes in camp. No trophies.

Take a First-Aid course at your local Red Cross chapter or fire station.

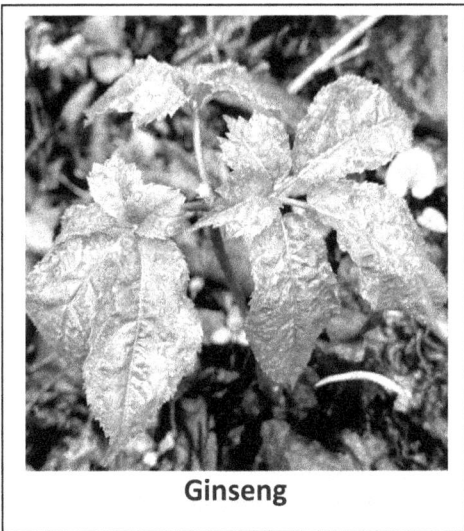

Ginseng

ii. HYGIENE

Hygiene is obviously the most personal aspect of backpacking. Afford yourself whatever supplies you deem necessary to fulfill your own needs and comfort. This is one of the few aspects of backpacking where weight/space considerations are waived. If it supports your hygiene needs and comfort, bring it!

Some items that I've found indispensable over the years:

- Metal poo trowel (1 per group)

    If packing out your human waste is impractical, make a direct deposit of your business into a hole dug 6- to 8-inches deep and +200' from running water, camp, trails and drainages.

- Small plastic shopping bags for:
  o Storing dirty/wet clothes and camp shoes in backpack
  o Use as a campsite trash bag

- o Packing out #2 waste (double-bagged in *Zip-lock* bag). Doggie poo cleanup bags work well for the initial grab.

- Wet wipes. Very handy when camping where water is scarce. Don't use to clean cookware/eating utensils.

- Pocket-sized solar shower – a luxury item that is worth its (low) weight in gold, especially in mild/warm weather camping trips exceeding two days.

Morel mushrooms

Appalachia's finest forest food

iii.   SAFETY

Strongly recommend studying navigation skills (compass use, what to do if lost, etc.). There are many excellent online and printed resources dedicated to this topic.

Group Size

There is some truth to the "strength in numbers" approach when it comes to backpacking. Campsite chores such as water and firewood gathering can be lightened, and individual pack weights can be reduced by eliminating the carrying of commonly-used items by multiple people.   Additionally, a larger group size affords a safer emergency response, especially if some in the party have to go for help while another stays behind to care for the injured/infirmed.

Therefore, I recommend a group size of no fewer than three. Four is more ideal for longer trips (3+ days) into deeper wilds.   Two is recommended only for shorter (length and duration) trips in familiar territory. Group sizes over four can diminish the "nature sanctity" factor. I personally find that large groups make for too much noise in general and diminish wildlife viewing opportunities, but obviously this is a personal preference. Find your sweet spot.

Everyone carries a whistle on their body. Some packs have these built-in but obviously are useless if not wearing the pack.

Learn the area's hunting season calendar. Wear a bright orange hunter safety vest or hat accordingly. Affix a bright orange item to the rear of your pack to become even more unmistakable to a hunter.

Conduct day hikes in groups of no fewer than two, ideally.

St. Mary's Lake – Glacier N.P., MT

a. Bears

When hiking in dense forest in bear country, regularly make a racket to avoid surprising an unsuspecting bear.

Carry bear-strength pepper spray and **learn how to use it properly.**

Keep pepper spray very handy as many bear encounters are of a surprise nature. Seconds count.

Studies have shown pepper spray to be a more effective bear deterrent than firearms.

Do not discharge bear spray in enclosed spaces (like your tent) unless ABSOLUTELY as a last resort. You will lose.

Keep a clean camp. Do NOT allow bears (or any animals) access to your food.

Let's bring some humor to bear … one evening at the camp fire, a young and curious backpacking neophyte asked if she should be worried about bears. With barely a pause (pardon the pun), my niece responded that there was nothing to fear because "it's not like bears know how to operate tent zippers". Mic drop.

~~~~~~~~~~~~~~~~~~~~~~~~~~~~~

The following is excerpted from the excellent guidance offered on the National Park Service website (nps.gov):

Each bear and each experience is unique; there is no single strategy that will work in all situations and that guarantees safety. Most bear encounters end without injury. Following some basic guidelines may help to lessen the threat of danger. Your safety can depend on your ability to calm the bear.

Always check with the nearest visitor center or backcountry office for the latest bear safety information.

If You Encounter a Bear:

- **Identify yourself** by talking calmly so the bear knows you are a human and not a prey animal. Remain still; stand your ground but slowly wave your arms. Help the bear recognize you as a human. It may come closer or stand on its hind legs to get a better look or smell. A standing bear is usually curious, not threatening.

- **Stay calm** and remember that most bears do not want to attack you; they usually just want to be left alone. Bears may bluff their way out of an encounter by charging and then turning away at the last second. Bears may also react defensively by woofing, yawning, salivating, growling, snapping their jaws, and laying their ears back. Continue to talk to the bear in low tones; this will help you stay calmer, and it won't be threatening to the bear. A scream or sudden movement may trigger an attack. Never imitate bear sounds or make a high-pitched squeal.

- **Pick up small children** immediately and remind them to stay calm and quiet. Do not make any loud noises or screams—the bear may think it's the sound of a prey animal. Slowly wave your arms above your head and tell the bear to back off. Do NOT run or make any sudden movements.

- **Hike and travel in groups**. Groups of people are usually noisier and smellier than a single person. Therefore, bears often become aware of groups of people at greater distances, and because of their cumulative size, groups are also intimidating to bears.

- **Make yourselves look as large as possible** (for example, move to higher ground).

- **Do NOT drop your pack** as it can provide protection for your back and prevent a bear from accessing your food.

- If the bear is stationary, **move away slowly and sideways**; this allows you to keep an eye on the bear and avoid tripping. Moving sideways is also non-threatening to bears.

- **Do NOT run**, but if the bear follows, stop and hold your ground. Bears can run as fast as a racehorse both uphill and down. Like dogs, they will chase fleeing animals.

- **Do NOT climb a tree**. Both grizzlies and black bears can climb trees.

- **Leave** the area or take a detour. If this is impossible, wait until the bear moves away. Always leave the bear an escape route.

- **Be especially cautious if you see a female with cubs**; never place yourself between a mother and her cub, and never attempt to approach them. The chances of an attack escalate greatly if she perceives you as a danger to her cubs.

Bear Attacks

Bear attacks are rare; most bears are only interested in protecting food, cubs, or their space. However, being mentally prepared can help you have the most effective reaction. Every situation is different, but below are guidelines on how brown bear attacks can differ from black bear attacks. Help protect others by reporting all bear incidents to the land unit manager ASAP. Above all, keep your distance from bears!

- **Brown/Grizzly Bears:** If you are attacked by a brown/grizzly bear, leave your pack on and **PLAY DEAD**. Lay flat on your stomach with your hands clasped behind your neck. Spread your legs to make it harder for the bear to turn you over. Remain still until the bear leaves the area. Fighting back usually increases the intensity of such attacks. However, if the attack persists, fight back vigorously. Use whatever you have at hand to hit the bear in the face.

- **Black Bears:** If you are attacked by a black bear, **DO NOT PLAY DEAD**. Fight back using any object available. Concentrate your kicks and blows on the bear's face and muzzle.

If any bear attacks you in your tent, or stalks you and then attacks, do NOT play dead - fight back! This kind of attack is very rare, but can be serious because it often means the bear is looking for food and sees you as prey.

Bear Pepper Spray

Proper behavior in bear country and understanding bear behavior can help to avoid dangerous situations for people and bears. Bear spray should be used as a last line of defense when dealing with bears- not immediately upon seeing one.

Bear pepper spray is only to be used defensively to stop an aggressive, charging, or attacking bear. Although it's used in the same manner you would use mace on an attacking person, bear pepper spray and human pepper spray are not the same. Make sure you select an EPA approved product that is specifically designed to stop aggressive bears. It is not a repellent so do not apply to your body or equipment.

+++ End of nps.gov bear safety excerpt +++

! Keep pepper spray out of reach of children !

Storing Pepper Spray

- Bear spray canisters are under high pressure and can explode in high temperatures, so store in a cool location out of the sun.

- When not backpacking, store in a secure, locking container. This is particularly important if you have kids or pets. Treat bear spray as the serious weapon that it is.

- Regularly check your spray's expiration date and replace vigilantly.

- Note that some national parks prohibit carrying bear spray. Check the regulations as part of your trip planning.

Handling Pepper Spray

- Ensure the plastic safety clip is on to avoid accidental discharge.

- Take the spray in your tent at bedtime. Place where it can be readily located in the dark. Run through the safety clip release and general operation process in your mind (i.e., be able to operate blindfolded). Nervous about using? Inert sprays are available for practicing.

Using Pepper Spray

1. **Using bear spray should be the last resort.** If you meet a bear, courteously exchange pleasantries then very quickly remove your spray from its holster and remove its safety clip, then perform the evasion guidance outlined in the *If You Encounter A Bear* section above to avoid conflict.

2. If you feel imminently threatened, take up a downwind position (i.e., any wind is blowing from your back, toward the bear)

3. Ensure that your group is behind you. Remind children to stay calm and quiet.

4. Firmly hold the canister extended in front of you with two hands (one on the trigger and one on the can)

5. Now the hardest part, which requires great discipline, mental training and nerves of steel ... before the bear reaches within ten yards (30 feet) of you (the sacred, invisible line in the sand), very quickly make note of

a landmark on this invisible perimeter (i.e., identify/estimate a rock, tree or log that is ~30' from your position). In this manner you can establish a "don't shoot until you can see the whites in their eyes" point – the point when you will discharge the canister should the bear cross it. Otherwise, it will be very difficult to resist prematurely discharging in a moment of understandable panic as the bear charges.

The ten yard discharge distance was established to accommodate the fact that bears sometimes do a fake charge, only to pull-back at the last moment. No need to discharge your precious canister until the bear has crossed your safety perimeter.

6. If the bear continues charging and crosses the sacred line, aim slightly downward to allow for high-pressure canister recoil, then discharge its full contents. Beware that it will empty in a mere few seconds, which further emphasizes the critical importance of mental preparation for bear encounters and pepper spray usage. Be a boy/girl scout and be prepared.

7. Spray in a zigzag pattern, moving your arms only ~6-12 inches from side-to-side and up-and-down to put a dense, volatile

pepper mist between the bear and yourself / group. If the bear still doesn't stop, aim for its face.

8. Hopefully the bear will halt its charge and retreat in a fit of great discomfort. Leave the area stat. You can change your soiled undies later.

9. Note: If two persons in your party are carrying bear spray, align beside one another and determine who will "shoot" first. The first discharge will hopefully deter the bear and the second canister will never be needed. But if the bear continues charging after the first canister discharge begins, the second person can then commence discharging their canister (aiming straight for the bear's head). This obviously requires tight planning as the execution of this tact occurs in mere seconds.

b. **Firearms**

If you're comfortable packing heat (and firearms are allowed where you're backpacking), then by all means pack it. There are plenty of small pistols that really deliver (recommendations are beyond the scope of this book).

Nobody should pack a firearm without disclosure to the group before departure. As obvious as it may sound, discuss its conditions of use.

While I've never packed a firearm, I've been on plenty of trips where others have and it definitely brought a sense of security. I'm not averse to firearms, and may someday pack one. It's clearly a personal decision.

San Jacinto Nat'l. Wilderness, CA

c. Emergency Communications

The decision to pack a reliable communications capability should be driven fundamentally by your risk tolerance. As well, a good rule of thumb is to pack a capability based on a given trip's distance from civilization; the further from help you get, the greater the need for such a device. In the end, it's a planning decision that your party should make.

A messaging device is a good choice. These dependably use communication satellites to send an email, SMS text or SOS message. Many options are available.

Mobile phone technology continues to advance rapidly, such as their use of satellite-based communications (does not use/require a cellular connection). Keep abreast of these developments and exploit accordingly.

Everything is for sale. Insurance options are available that include being rescued via a medivac helicopter. Prepare to take out a second mortgage though.

2. ASSEMBLE / PACK

Aside from the innate backpacking rewards outlined in the introduction, count as a success if you return from a trip and find that you used everything in your pack (First-Aid kit notwithstanding). This guide was written to support such success to the greatest possible extent.

Use *Appendix E – Packing Checklist* as your guide. Supplement the assorted *Luxury Items* at your discretion, paced mainly by your target loaded pack weight and your hedonistic tendencies.

At home, layout and group your items by the six major categories listed in *Appendix E*. If possible, do a final "buddy cross-check" to ensure that nothing is missed or duplicated.

After a lifetime of using countless various clothing items made of seemingly every known material, I've settled on a core set that have stood the test of time and represent the greatest value in terms of cost, durability, performance and comfort.

- Remember that the main goal is to stay dry. Sweating is the enemy.

- Big fan of nylon pants w/zip-off shorts (especially for milder weather trips). Durable and quick-drying. A small amount (<20%) of cotton in the fabric mix is OK.

- Avoid junky, lightweight pants fabric

- Double material at the knees (and the tushy, optionally) is valuable

- Good pants are well worth the money. *Fjallraven* brand recommended.

- Avoid 100% cotton clothing items – in any season. Forget blue jeans. Although tough, they're slow drying, offer poor insulation when wet and restrict movement/flexibility.

• Wool-synthetic blends are durable and warm, even when wet

• Dead air is the best insulator. Any two-layer top garment having an inner-lining with a waffle/perforated/mesh fabric design will create air pockets and trap heat better.

• Invest in a quality waterproof rain coat that is made of breathable material, has a hefty hood bill and has a cut that ideally fully covers your bum. Avoid rubberized material, which is heavy and sweaty. A rain coat should be sized while wearing several layers, and oversized is far better than undersized. Pack it always, unless on a 2-3 day trip with a clear forecast, in which case a cheap pocket poncho should be packed instead.

• Use quality socks made specifically for backpacking. *Darn Tuff* brand is very fine. Pack one spare pair.

• Wear a belt. Recommend the indestructible nylon webbing type. Multi-use: tourniquet, a place to carry your survival knife, tying up captured bears, etc.

- Always pack a pair of gloves during Fall-Winter-Spring

Layers, layers, layers!

<u>This cannot be overemphasized</u>. Layering will beat a single garment approach every time as a single garment will typically be heavier, bulkier, less comfortable/flexible, more difficult to pack and less versatile (more difficult to regulate body temperature). Layers can quickly be adjusted to accommodate multiple conditions.

o **Summer**

  ▪ Nylon tee. One or more, based on trip length.

  ▪ Long-sleeved, *Henley*-type pullover having 2-layer fabric made of mostly synthetic material

- "No see-um" bug netting for head (as conditions warrant). Pack if in doubt.

o **Spring & Fall**

- Two long-sleeved, double-layered pullovers

- Down-filled vest, having a waist draw-cord and extended bottom length at rear/back. A *Thinsulate*-type (man-made) insulation is a fine alternative.

- Silk long johns (long bottoms and long-sleeved, pullover top). Nothing compares to the comfort, warmth and durability of silk as the next-to-body (base) layer, plus it weighs (and packs down to) virtually nothing. Recommend wearing to bed, and also wearing as the base layer whenever additional warmth is needed in camp. Not recommended for wearing while hiking, except during cold weather.

o **Winter** (see also *Winter Camping* sect. 4.vii)

- Save for the rain coat and zip-off pants, bring all of the Spring and Fall items above, plus a hooded, waterproof shell having a generous cut, a full-length zipper, generous inside and outside pockets and low-profile (un-bulky) synthetic insulation

- Avoid bulky down coats, especially in the backcountry where they won't stand up to abrasions when hiking off-trail. Too risky if garment fails. Loose fitting layers will always outperform a single garment.

- 100% wool, wool blends and fleece are suitable alternatives for under layers

- Full-length, insulated balaclava

- Insulated ski bibs (worn over long johns) work very well in winter conditions. Their elastic snow cuffs at the leg bottoms eliminate the need for separate gaiters.

- Add a pair of insulated mittens. Austrian boiled wool *Dachstein* mittens worn under a weatherproof shell are noteworthy. Sizes run on the small side.

- Silk glove liners add additional insulation and are useful when dexterity is needed (e.g., cooking/eating).

Savage River State Forest, MD

A Few Words on Hats …

NEVER go without a hat. Consider it an essential survival item. Choose which hat(s) to pack based on conditions (sun exposure, wind, temperature, precipitation):

- Spring/Summer - Insulated beanie (wool exterior with liner made of itch-less material)
- Fall/Winter - Insulated balaclava (wool/synthetic combo)
- All seasons - Silk balaclava. Also useful as an under-layer if you're prone to wool itching.

In the spring, summer and fall seasons, I always pack a long-billed sun visor type hat (has a bill only; not a baseball cap). This lightweight item provides eye shading, some protection of the face from the sun and keeps eyeglasses dry in drizzle/light rain.

For full sun exposure and hiking at altitude (above ~9K' in North America where UV rays are potent), take a lightweight, nylon "desert hat" that affords full face and neck coverage, and has a high UV protection rating (SPF 50+).

- **Hiking Boots**

  o   Boots are arguably THE most important item. Proper fitting, comfortable and durable hiking boots are essential to successful trips.

  o   IMPORTANT: Choose boots that cover and protect the ankles. Don't deviate.

  o   Don't buy without trying on in store

  o   Sample a variety of makes and models, wearing the weight/type of socks that you plan to use on the trail

  o   Sample wearing a weighted pack (an option typically offered by reputable purveyors)

  o   Aim for boots with removable insoles for better drying and odor control post-trip

  o   Consider using *Superfeet* brand insoles, unless the boot in mind won't accept them (i.e., has its own built-in and un-removable insoles)

My first four decades of backpacking used the traditional boots having all-leather uppers and a Norwegian type of welt affixing their *Vibram* soles to their uppers. Good stuff for sure, and no regrets. However, recently I've been using the *Solomon* brand boot, a composite construction made of nylon/leather uppers welded to the soles. They're holding up well after 5 years and they fit like a glove from the get-go, with no breaking-in period required and never a blister. Their down side is that they can't be re-soled.

Take your time on this important purchase. The bottom line is that there are many high-quality boots on the market. Resist skimping and you'll do well.

Get on the good foot!

Virgin River, Zion N.P., UT

- **Camp Shoes**

Huge fan of camp shoes. Although not an absolutely essential item, slipping into a comfortable pair of dry and warm camp shoes after a long day's hike is sublime, especially if one has wet or damp feet. Also, these are very nice to slip into upon rising from your shelter each morning. *Teva* brand is recommended, but many good options exist.

Seek lightweight, pull-on type shoes having firm soles and full coverage (heel, toes and tops of feet covered). Think substantive enough for light duty (e.g., firewood foraging, strolls near campsite).

Absolutely no flip-flops.
Although, plenty swear by the beefier and light hiking sandals offering far better foot protection than flip-flops.

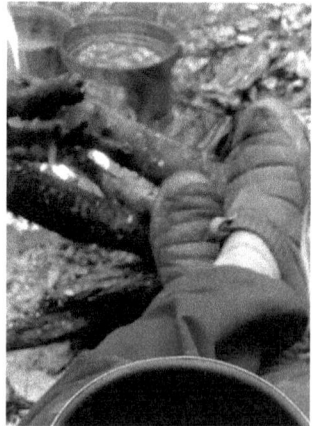

Selecting

A proper fitting, comfortable and durable pack is critical to a successful trip

Do not skimp. Take your time with this expensive and important purchase.

Don't buy without trying on. Solicit the help of an experienced salesperson who especially understands how packs can be adjusted for best fit.

Sample a variety of makes and models, fully loaded with special weights typically offered in-store.

Like shopping for the right boots, you'll know when the pack for you is on your back. Put it back if it doesn't feel right.

It's better to have a slightly oversized pack capacity than undersized

What makes a good backpack?

- Internal frame type. My first 30 years of backpacking used external frame packs. While these have since been passed down and remain fully functional, the switch to an internal frame pack was a marked improvement. I'll likely never go back.

- Can accommodate a water bladder / hydration system, although not considered essential

- Comes with a rain cover. Buy one if it doesn't, and ensure that it's oversized.

- Has ample external attachment loops and load cinching straps

- Has multiple interior compartments with separate access. Favored over the single chamber (and typically top-loading) style.

- Has external side, front and top compartments, all having zippered access

- Has a detachable "hood" doubling as a fanny pack for light day hikes

- Affords some degree of torso ventilation

Using Your Backpack

Never lift your loaded pack by its shoulder straps. Instead, always use the sturdy, special-purpose lifting/hanging loop located at the pack's top-rear-center. To mount your pack:

1. Loosen the pack's shoulder straps and hip belt

2. Grab the lifting strap by both hands and lift/place the bottom of pack onto your bent right knee. It's easier if you can first place your right foot onto a slightly elevated surface (e.g., low vehicle bumper, log, or rock).

3. Gripping the lifting strap by your left hand (over-handed); release your right hand from the lifting strap then slide your right arm through the right shoulder strap and

grab the lifting strap (under-handed) with your right hand

4. Using both hands on the lifting strap, swing the pack around and onto your slightly bent-over back

5. Release your left hand's grip from the lifting strap then slide your left arm into the left shoulder strap

6. Release your right hand's grip from the lifting strap then partially tighten both shoulder straps to secure the pack to your back

7. Attach the waist belt; tighten

8. Stand up; adjust all straps

9. The waist belt and shoulder straps should feel snug and not tight, and the load should feel evenly distributed

Tips

Load heavy items nearest top of pack (e.g., tent, food, fuel); lightest items nearest bottom (e.g., sleeping bag, clothing)

Pack quick-reach items in outside pack pockets (map, raincoat, pack rain cover, snacks, phone/camera, water, headlamp). I've found that loading all such items into a single pocket if possible is ideal. For example, the pocket that on most internal frame packs is located on the top (i.e., the flap covering the main upper internal chamber).

Attempt to adhere to the pack target weight general rules of thumb outlined above in the *Getting Started* section. Once fully packed, first weigh yourself at home without the pack and then with it. Adjust your contents accordingly to stay within a reasonable pack target weight.

How much your target weight can be exceeded is foremost a personal choice based on how much you feel that you can comfortably carry vis-à-vis the trip's anticipated rigor factors (i.e., your physical condition, distance to be travelled, trip duration and difficulty level). Slogging a heavy pack in sand or on steep terrain is entirely different than lollygagging along on a level and clear trail.

Experience will be your best teacher. Err on the side of conservatism though ... an overloaded pack has greatly diminished the joys of many trips, especially in my early years. Leave the machismo at home.

Attach bear spray to outside of pack in a very-quick-to-reach spot (i.e., reach with no pack dismount).

Don't trust the mesh water bottle pockets typically located low on the outside of packs. Secure cargo stored in these pockets using straps.

Sand Beach Lake, Rocky Mountain N.P., CO

3. HIKE

i. Before Hitting the Trail

Set expectations. Each day, jointly review the route, distance, destination and schedule.

Discuss bear encounter plan with group.

Do some stretching exercises.

Put phones in airplane and mute mode, thank you. If hiking off trail, don't carry phone in pants pocket. Ever.

Use an eyeglass lanyard.   Avoid serious damage to your eyeglasses from having them knocked off of your face by an unsuspecting branch or an insect swat. Please heed this critical advice.

Store wallet and vehicle keys (attached) inside pack. Don't take your wallet or vehicle keys if possible.

Break-in your new boots by hiking at least a few miles at home with some load on your back.

48

Avoid "head down" trudging. After all, backpacking is every bit as much about the journey as it is about the destination. Awareness of surroundings is essential to your safety and enjoyment. Strive for a state of "chilled alertness" at all times. You can have both elements simultaneously with practice.

Look up frequently, enjoy the view and scan the trail and horizon for wildlife viewing opportunities and threats (e.g., approaching storms, snakes, bears).

Like the good driving practice, use your "rear-view mirror" by occasionally turning around and surveying the rear.

Increase your safety by stepping over, and not on, obstacles (rocks, downed trees, etc.).

Take occasional micro-breaks, short enough to be beneficial but not disruptive to the group's hiking pace. Remain standing, leave your pack on and sip some water.

Regularly check with one another and take longer breaks accordingly, especially when hiking in tougher conditions like high altitude, heat, cold, long distances and rough/steep terrain.

Wrap a joint at the onset of discomfort (but don't smoke it until you get to camp).

Avoid heavy sweating, especially in cool / cold weather. Remember: dry = warm in cool weather; dry = cool in warm weather.

Wasatch Front. UT

When hiking in dense forest cover, keep a safe distance from the person in front of you to avoid tree branch backlash.

If anyone in your posse has an arachnid phobia (fear of spiders) and you're in a forest, hike in a single file line and have the lead swipe up regularly using their hiking pole to clear webs.

Treat blisters as soon as they appear. Cut a square of moleskin twice as large as the blister diameter. Fold in half. Use scissors to cut a semi-circle (centered on the fold) that is <u>slightly larger than half</u> of the blister diameter. Unfold moleskin, center hole over blister (blister shouldn't touch moleskin). Cut a gauze piece slightly larger than the moleskin hole. Center the gauze over the moleskin hole. Tape the gauze and moleskin to dry skin.

If you experience painful itching skin after encountering the Appalachian stinging nettle plant, a natural antidote is to break the hollow, translucent stem of a jewelweed plant (orange flowers) and rub its juices on the area.

Fortunately these two plants like moist conditions, and are often found growing together.

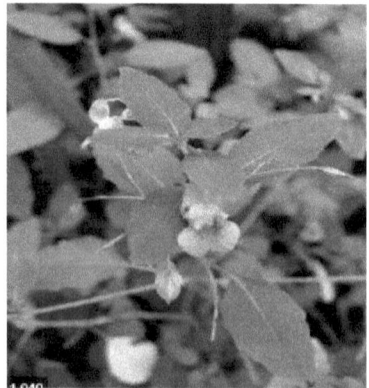

Jewelweed

Stream Crossings

- Keep one foot firmly planted at all times

- Take small steps

- Shuffle along in the stream where possible

- Step over and not on objects where possible

- Use your hiking pole to create a more stable tri-pod affect

- Avoid leaping. It's far better to get wet boots and feet than to risk injury from leaping.

- Good safety rule of thumb: if you can't see the stream bottom, don't cross if your route allows an alternative

Hiking on Steep Inclines (on or off trail)

Take small steps. Longer strides are inherently less stable and are more prone to stretching-related injuries caused when attempting to recover from a sudden slip or fall.

- **Going Uphill** - lean in slightly. It's not hard to fall backward carrying a pack.

- **Going Downhill** - lean slightly back. It's not hard to tumble forward carrying a pack. Point toes slightly outward, providing more surface traction and less slippage potential. If descending too steeply to comfortably approach head-on:
  - Re-distribute the load to your shoulders by loosening waist belt slightly and tightening shoulder straps slightly
  - Slow down. Traverse with feet planted parallel with slope with each side-step down.
  - Re-plant hiking pole on the downhill side before each step
  - Alternate the approach occasionally by rotating body 180 degrees

4. CAMP

i. CAMPSITE SELECTION

What makes a good campsite?

- It is scenic and not within eyesight/earshot of other campsites

- Offers some wind protection (reducing stray camp fire embers risk and wind chill cooling)

- Contains an ample supply of the 3 D's of firewood: downed, dead and dry

- Does not contain nearby "widow maker" hazards represented by falling dead trees and limbs

- Provides treatable running water within a reasonable distance

- Is ideally below the tree line

- Is kept tidy by its occupants

- Ideally, contains no signs of occupancy when selected and vacated

Options   include   simple   tarps,   covered hammocks and the good old-fashioned tent. I prefer and recommend the latter as it:

• Provides a small degree of warmth

• Affords the best wind protection

• Is the driest option

• Is bug and snake proof

• Provides a sense of security (albeit false)

• Is the most private

• Is the most comfortable for hunkering down in inclement weather

• Is lightweight considering the benefits outlined above (a one-person tent can weigh under two pounds)

• Provides clean, dry and solid flooring for deflating/packing air mattress, and for packing/compressing sleeping bag and clothing bag

What makes a good tent?

- Has adequate storage pockets, ideally in both sidewalls and ceiling

- Its zippered entrance is located on a side wall and not on an end. A tent suitable for two or more persons should have a zippered door on each side wall.

- Has a ventilated (screen/mesh fabric) ceiling (and possibly some of its walls) to allow "breathing" and minimize condensation

- Has a one-piece, tub-style floor having continuous sidewalls that extend up from the floor at least six inches

- Has full rain fly coverage. I.e., the fly extends ideally 4"-6" beyond the tent's footprint and, when tautly pitched, the rain fly does not come into contact with the tent walls and ceiling.

- The fly offers a vestibule. This provides invaluable, protected storage space outside the tent's door(s) for camp shoes, hiking boots, pants, dogs, etc.

- Has a few ceiling tabs for hanging things

- Has glow-in-the-dark guy lines

- Ideally is free-standing, meaning that after the tent (without its rain fly) is pitched (poles secured into the floor's corners) but before any tent pegs are driven, it can be picked up by its poles as a single unit. This makes for easy tent floor shake-out cleaning during tear-down. Not an imperative feature, but nice to have nonetheless.

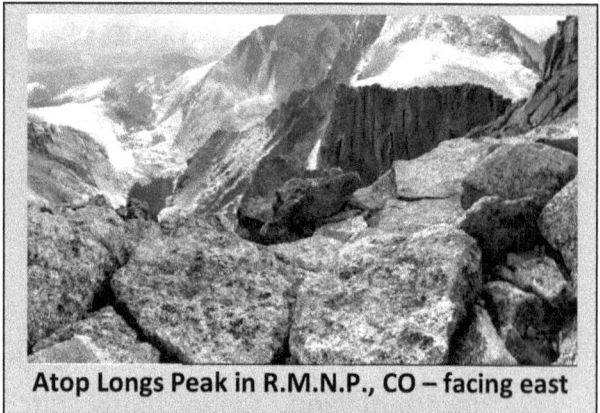

Atop Longs Peak in R.M.N.P., CO – facing east

The Fungus Amongus

Shelter Tips

Use 3-sided, metal "groundhog" style pegs for securing anything into the ground.

Avoid expensive ground cloths ("footprints") sold by tent manufacturers. Use inexpensive 6ML (minimum) plastic instead. Cut to fit 2" shy of tent floor's footprint, allowing (after the ground cloth is centered under the tent floor) a 1" ground cloth edge buffer that helps to prevent water from seeping/wicking onto the underside of the tent floor.

Pack your tent bag in this order: 1.) Poles and stakes (usually have their own bag). 2.) Rain fly. 3.) Tent. Stuff the rain fly and tent into the bag. Do not fold as this reputedly can cause fabric strain/weakness at the folds.

Select a tent pitch site that is as level as possible. Even the slightest incline can send you steadily toward the downhill end by morning (if not sooner). This truly sucks. Try to avoid.

Step on the entire area where the tent will be pitched, removing any appreciable (especially sharp) protrusions. Your air mattress will mask any minor surface imperfections.

Do not pitch your tent/shelter within forty feet of a camp fire. Pitch even further away, if possible. Ignore this advice and your tent's rain fly will assuredly eventually suffer burn holes, if not a worse fate, from wind-borne camp fire embers.

One simply can't comfortably stay in a tent for hours on end, no matter how good the book or how fine the partner. And so if the weather forecast is dicey (>50% chance of precipitation), it's worth carrying a "hangout" tarp that's large enough to comfortably accommodate your party size (when configured as a lean-to). Or do load sharing and have two persons each carry a smaller tarp (and cordage) that can be configured as one.

Once you've had enough trips using those ubiquitous cheap blue tarps, recommend upgrading to a high-quality, low-weight professional backpacking tarp made of silicone-nylon laminate

Regardless of the tarp type, don't forget the spare (paracord) cordage. Paracord is a slim and very strong nylon rope with 7-9 inner strands of nylon. Composed of 2-3 threads each, the inner strands can be unraveled for unlimited creative uses. Recommend perusing the web to learn as many as possible.

Carry a simple field repair kit per *Appendix E - Packing Checklist*. Bring your MacGyver-like acumen.

Learn (and practice) the basic knots shown in *Appendix C*.

**Taking a break after 17 miles …
or was it 20?**

Maroon Bells Wilderness, CO

A camp fire is one of backpacking's many rewards and, while not absolutely essential, having a fire cannot be beat. Consider yourself fortunate if you can have one.

**MacGruder Corridor / Nez Perce Trail
Selway-Bitterroot Wilderness, MT**

Assess the risks. Understand the current fire danger threat level assigned to the particular land unit by its manager. Accordingly, make your decision to build a fire or not, or even to go into the area in the first place.

Don't build a fire if you can't properly extinguish it with water. Use dirt or sand in a pinch. Douse then stir. Repeat until the fire is a mere corpse of its former self: dead and cold.

Collect firewood using a folding / locking handsaw like the Japanese-style that cuts on the pull stroke. *Silky* brand is awesome. Many good brands are available. Figure one saw for every two persons in your party.

A hatchet is nice to have but not recommended. It's hard to justify the weight-to-benefit value.

Pack in your cook set an indispensable single glove that fits your weak hand, made preferably of soft goat leather. Use for fire maintenance and cooking chores.

a. Preparing for a Fire

• Clear an area at least one foot beyond the planned fire's diameter

• Avoid large fires. Target an ~18-inch diameter fire base (larger only if winter camping).

- Before prepping the evening's fire, gather and cover enough kindling and firewood to start the next morning's fire. It's not pleasant to be the first to rise on a cold and potentially wet morning and have to forage for wood. Politely yet firmly inform your party of the purpose of this sacred pile.

- Avoid rimming a fire with rocks, especially sedimentary rocks found near a stream. Sooner or later you will be surprised (and put at great risk) by the loud and dangerous explosion resulting from steam heating.

- It's far better to dig a shallow (~4"deep) pit than to rim your fire with rocks. Although, it's OK to use a few rocks temporarily to provide stability for a grate while cooking over fire.

- Use damp / rotting logs as wind screens if needed. Alternative: soak a few logs in stream/lake for an hour to create logs for this purpose.

- Gather a fist-sized tinder bundle comprised of the smallest and driest branch tips available, ideally taken from dead evergreen branches. Alternative tinder:

  - Flaky, dry bark from dead and standing trees. Think paper birch bark.

  - Dead grass, dry leaves, pine cones, dead wood shavings

  - Man-made items, although not nearly as rewarding:

    - Store-bought fire starter sticks
    - Piece of fake log made for fireplaces
    - Dryer lint smeared w/petroleum jelly
    - Good ol' paper/light cardboard

- Gather a bundle of twigs ~1/4″ in diameter. Use some of these to lay-up five overlapping courses / rows to create a square *Lincoln Log*-type structure having a ~10″ inside diameter. Will provide an excellent air feed.

- Gather an armful of larger firewood. Divide and conquer: send the rest of your party to gather the wood needed for the evening. Strive for pieces that are less than 8" in diameter.

- Place tinder into the log cabin

structure and apply flame/spark

- Steadily feed using the remaining small twigs, then progressively larger wood. Flame on!

Tips

Don't waste precious wood trying to build an all-nighter fire at bedtime. It never works, it's less safe and it's not worth wasting precious firewood. At best, you're lucky to have a few coals in the morning sufficient to light a fire using tinder.

Don't waste your energy (and saw blade sharpness) by sawing individual log lengths. Instead, saw logs into 3' lengths then burn in half to create two logs.

Always pack multiple fire starters:

o Butane lighter

o Windproof / waterproof matches

o Create super hot ignition sparks by striking your survival knife's thick backside across a ferro rod. Do not strike on the sharp side of the blade shaft. Foolproof, but requires some practice (at home).

Leave No Trace

Don't pick the area clean. Spread out and scavenge wood from nearby instead.

Don't leave saw marks (sawn stumps or sawn downed wood). Leave no trace and use the entire wood piece.

Thoroughly extinguish your fire with water. Distribute excess DEAD ashes in woods using cook set pans.

Disguise fire pit by filling / covering to ground level using leaves and woody debris.

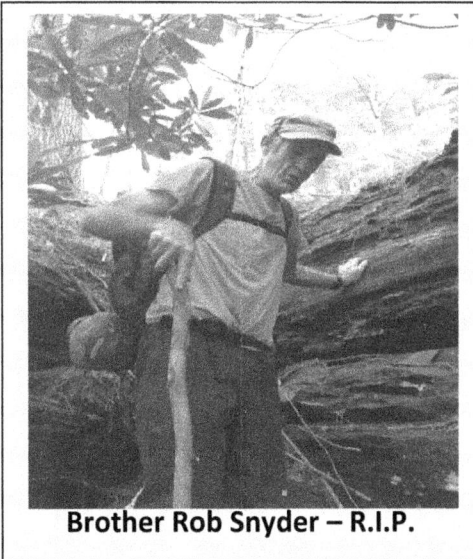

Brother Rob Snyder – R.I.P.

iv.   WATER

Access to treatable water is of foremost importance. Plan accordingly.

Carrying excessive amounts of water is brutal.

Assuming you have access to running, treatable water throughout your trip, carry one quart of filtered/treated water at all times. Increase the quantity carried as water availability decreases.

Figure on using 2 quarts of <u>drinking</u> water per person per day.

Always pack inexpensive and effective water treatment tablets as a water filter backup. Store in First-Aid kit.

Use collapsible water transport vessels (e.g., dromedary bag) for gathering water for campsite needs. Recommend carrying a one-gallon capacity per person.

Keep close tabs on which vessels contain filtered/sterilized water and which do not.

Filtering Water

For a party of four or less on a trip of three days or less, one water filter is recommended. *Sawyer* brand works well. Lightweight, efficient and compact. Pack its cleaning mechanism. Bring a spare filter squeeze bag on longer trips.

Clean filter immediately after every trip.

Do not allow water filter to freeze.

Don't use water filter to directly process cloudy/dirty water. Pass such water through a clean cloth first to filter out large particles. Allow bottle to settle for at least an hour before passing through water filter.

DO NOT EVER drink un-filtered/un-boiled/un-treated water. If you need persuaded of this, seek the testimony of someone who has endured giardia.

As an alternative to using a water filter (and assuming camp fire access), sterilize water by bringing to a covered, rolling boil for 1 minute. Boil for 3 minutes at elevations above 6,500'. Let boiled water cool then store in sanitized containers having tight-fitting lids. Such boiling kills giardia.

San Juan National Forest, CO

v. FOOD

a. Planning

Truism: food tastes more sumptuous in the wild.

Access to a campfire expands the menu options. Devise accordingly.

Cooking over a stove limits you mostly to pan and hot water-based meals, which is not inherently a bad thing.

Devise a food load-sharing (carrying) plan.

Think dense food items having a high nutritional and caloric value.

Avoid light, bulky foods hogging pack space.
Avoid foods requiring complicated preparation. I once hauled oil and made falafel. Bad idea. Ditto for the rack of lamb that I once tried over a camp fire, which tasted great, but what a mess.

Think minimal cleanup and waste stream.

Eat as much fresh food as possible.

Beware of (some) high-sodium freeze-dried foods.

Always double-bag foods containing liquid.

b. Recommendations

- Hard cheeses keep for days unrefrigerated
- Nuts, seeds and dried fruits are a must. Make your own trail mix at home.
- It's hard to beat a foil-wrapped potato baked in camp fire coals. Double-wrap; place directly on coals; flip and rotate after 20 minutes. Poke with knife to test doneness.
- Pack some sweet treats. Surprise the kids with S'mores.
- Non-perishable food options:
  - PBJs
  - Tuna/sardines
  - Energy bars; Climber's energy gels
  - Jerky/cured meats
  - Bagels, apples, oatmeal

- Ramen noodles, granola
- Soup mixes made of dehydrated vegetables and quick-cooking legumes (make your own at home)

- Hot drinks = comfort! Pack ground coffee and a reusable filter, teas, cocoa, honey.

c. Dinner Ideas

Dinner Day #1: Prior to departing, freeze the entrees in double-sealed bags. Limit to one-pot meals (e.g., stews) if cooking is limited to using a stove. For camp fire options, freeze meats for grilling or ... lay out a double layer of aluminum foil, apply generous coating of grapeseed oil, add salmon (skin side down) then sliced vegetables and seasoning. Fold a sturdy, top-center seam then freeze in sealable bag. Pack the bag away from the part of pack nearest your body to delay over-thawing before evening. Lay thawed foil packet over hot coals or grate for ~20 minutes, eating directly from package for a no fuss, no cleanup meal. Pairs well with Pinot Noir.

Dinner Day #2: Think non-perishable yet fresh food like vacuum-sealed tomato sauce (frozen the night before departure), Parmesan cheese block, penne pasta, uncut fresh peppers and onion. Cut veges in camp then sauté in oil in smallest pan, cover and keep warm. Cook pasta in largest pan; drain well then add sauce and re-heat. Add veges and stir well. Plate then top with freshly-shaven cheese. Bon appetit!

Food for days three and beyond typically transition into the realm of non-perishable items, including freeze-dried foods which, although expensive, offer many choices with greatly-improved quality in recent years.

Practice deferred gratification by enjoying that fresh fruit on day three ... or four.

Ahhhh ... venison tenderloin!

As part of setting up your campsite, string a rope that will secure your food bags, bear-proof canisters and trash bag overnight.

Affix a small rock to your special 30' rope length; throw it over the part of a stiff branch that is 10' out from the tree's trunk. Hang items 10' from the ground.

Even if you don't use a bear canister, also hang your food and trash if your camp will be unattended for any length of time.

Keep food in a cinching bag for ready hanging.

Marmots, chipmunks and squirrels will rob you blind, and right before your eyes. Zip it!

Food Thief Extraordinaire

Use metal (titanium or stainless) eating utensils. Durable and easy to clean.

Invest in titanium, two-piece, comes-apart spatula / tong combo, and a sturdy, metal pot lifter.

Cookset / Pots

- A cook set having a 2-quart and a 1.5-quart pot will suffice for a group of four
- Use titanium (preferred) or stainless steel
- Avoid aluminum and coated surfaces
- Seek a nesting cookset with a storage bag and a single lid that fits either pot
- Use lid as a plate / prep space

Avoid pots with built-in / collapsible handles. They're typically flimsy, unwieldy and hot to handle. Instead, use a pot lifter and glove.

Cups can cover a majority of food and beverage serving needs. Use a metal, double-walled, insulated cup with a lid. Having a second, wide-mouthed, *Lexan*-type plastic cup with a large handle is useful.

A small, unbreakable plate can be useful, depending on meal plans.

Invest in a quality fire grate, preferably made of titanium and having a tight mesh surface, collapsible legs and a storage sack. Well worth the weight.

Optionally, pack a small, thin, plastic cutting board (luxury item).

Items to store inside cook set:

o Multi-purpose, bio-degradable castile soap stored in a 2 oz. plastic bottle w/tight-fitting cap (e.g., hotel shampoo bottle). A few drops will do each job.
o Scour pad
o Dish towel, pot lifter, glove
o 30' of paracord to hang food and trash bags overnight
o Spare lighter, small multi-purpose tool, spices / seasonings / condiment packets

Cooking over open fire versus gas stoves

If your trip is assured to have a camp fire and the forecast is clear and not overly windy, skip the gas stove.

While gas stoves are relatively lightweight, highly efficient, dependable, and provide an instant and relatively controllable flame, they're not an absolutely essential item with camp fire availability.

Savage River State Forest, MD

Many swear by a gas stove and wouldn't camp without one, so this comes down to another weight-versus-benefit decision. Although, the joy of cooking over a camp fire feeds the primal spirit and borders on the art form.

If you favor a stove regardless, it's hard to beat the affordable *MSR Pocket Rocket*, which packs quite small. Pack one stove for every two persons. On shorter trips (one or two nights) pack one stove and one 8-ounce fuel canister for every two persons.

A life well lived:
backpacking w/grand-nephew/nieces

On extended trips (three or more nights) using gas stoves, plan on <u>each</u> person carrying an 8-ounce fuel canister. This is one item whose value far exceeds its relatively small weight penalty. Do not skimp on fuel supplies.

b. Cooking By Camp Fire

To build a bed of cooking coals (and if not packing charcoal), start your camp fire at least one hour prior to chow time.

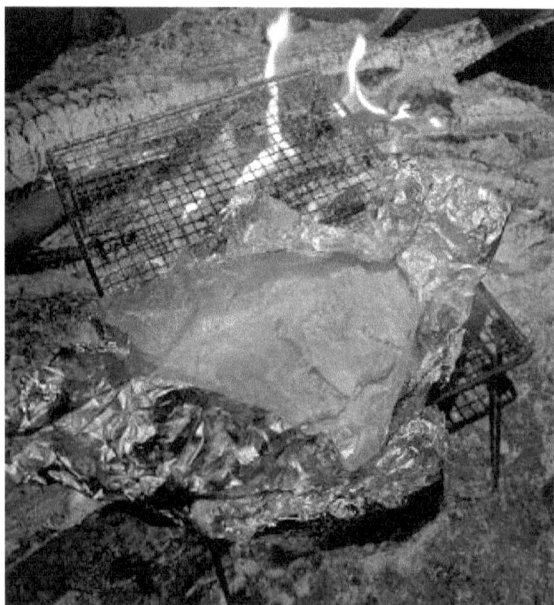

Steamed and grilled pheasant breast

Cook to the side of the main fire body by pulling some coals beneath the cooking grate. Add charcoal if using.

Have spare twigs on hand to maintain a small but steady cooking flame. Pencil-sized is ideal.

c. Cooking Tips

* <u>NEVER</u> hold anything into which hot liquid is being poured

* Keep children at a curious yet safe distance from the cooking area (camp fire and/or stove)

* Use a high flash-point cooking oil such as grapeseed

* Secure your pet prior to meal prep and during dining

* Avoid placing pots and grates over raging flames. Metal (even titanium) can deform

* Clean stubborn dirty pots initially with pine boughs/needles or river silt/small stones

- Charcoal is a luxury item and a wonderful thing to have if your first evening's meal requires grilling
  - Choose the lighter "true wood pieces" type over the heavier compressed wood briquettes
  - A one-gallon *Zip-lock* bag full is plenty
  - Place over camp fire coals to light
  - Avoid products containing lighter fluid

Note tiny mushroom atop host

- **Toiletries** (also see *Hygiene* section above)

  - Toothbrush/paste, floss, lip balm, tissues
  - Wet wipes - very handy when camping where water is scarce. Don't use to clean cookware/eating utensils.
  - Indispensable, multi-purpose, *compressed towlettes (search online)*:
    - Tiny, biodegradable pellets expand to 6″ x 8.5″ towlettes using a few drops of water (or spit in a pinch)
    - 10 fit nicely into a round waterproof match case
    - Hypoallergenic, soft and scent-free
    - Disposable yet reusable, can be rinsed many times
    - TP substitute (use 2-3 per BM)

- Hand towel

- Prescriptions, and any OTC meds not listed in *Appendix A - First Aid Kit Contents*

- LED headlamp having red lamp and strobe options. Use red lamp to preserve night vision, e.g., when reading a sky map during stargazing.

- o Install fresh batteries before each trip
- o On longer trips (three or more nights) take extra batteries and a spare headlamp. Phone light doesn't count as a spare.

- Metal trowel (one per group)

- Spare contact lenses, saline solution

- Personal bandages/supports (e.g., knee brace)

- Hat(s)

- Sunglasses

- Bandana (many uses, e.g., sweat band, tourniquet, wash cloth, 1st stage filter for murky water)

- Eyeglass lanyard. **Imperative.** You can't afford to lose/damage your absolutely vital eyeglasses.

- Survival knife, having:
  - Sheath for knife storage and slot for waist belt mounting
  - Full-tang construction
  - ~8-10" total length (avoid folding style knives)
  - Stainless or carbon-steel blade
  - Built-in ferro rod (fire starter) and blade sharpener

- Swiss-army pocket knife. Carry the smallest model made (small blade, scissors, file, screwdriver, metal tweezers).

Telluride Canyon, CO

The following items are considered non-essential. Your decision to carry these is subjective and is based solely on your desires and needs, and the decision to carry one or more of these items is typically driven by total pack weight objectives. Obviously, the shorter a trip is (in length, not duration), the more of these items can be carried since you won't be packing the extra weight as far. It's a trade-off that you get to decide.

- Lightweight, collapsible **chair**. I consider this as a borderline essential item, and always pack it. Choose a product having a shock-corded metal pole frame and a one-piece synthetic material as its seat/back. Amazingly strong and lightweight. Tonic for a tired body after a long day's trek. Highly recommended.

- Three-quarter length, ¼" thick dense (closed-cell) foam or folding eggshell-type **ground pad**. Relatively impervious to dirt.

OK, if you're packing a chair then why also bring a pad? Because sometimes ya wanna stretch your back or just watch the clouds roll by, beside the camp fire and in a fully prostrate position.

Also serves as extra insulation beneath your air mattress in cold weather, a backup to air mattress failure and a comfy space to plop yourself while cooking. Amazingly, I've been carrying the same *Ensolite* type of foam pad for over forty years. While admittedly now an unsightly and battle-scarred patchwork of the original material and duct tape, it has become my most prized and sentimental piece of gear.

Recommend rolling up and strapping on horizontally to the outside bottom of pack. Strap on vertically if bushwhacking in thick underbrush.

- **Electronics**

  o Music – ear buds/media device/small Bluetooth speaker. Be sensitive to your camp mate's sentiments regarding broadcasting music. Some may find offensive. Strike a balance.

  o Battery backup and various device charging cable(s)

  o Portable solar charger (min. 30W capacity) on trips more than three days

  o Battery-powered LED string lights for camp

- **Adult beverages** (no glass!)

  o Wine – pour at home into collapsible, special-purpose wine bladder that holds one 750ML bottle and weighs 1.6# full

  o Spirits – recommend using a lightweight titanium flask

  o Beer – freeze to half-solid at home; wrap in aluminum foil; pack in koozy. 12oz. = 3/4#.

- 1-to 2-gallon pocket-sized solar shower. Packs very small and works surprisingly well. Its trickle does the job. Handy for washing hands and doing dishes, too. Recommended for warm weather trips exceeding two days.

  Fill bag. Lay bag in sun for a few hours. Enjoy.

- Low-profile, collapsible table

- Reading material (aside from this book)

- Hammock (and rope/webbing/hooks for hanging). Heavy and heavenly.

- Hydration bladder / hose. Fits into special sleeve in backpack, with ready- access drinking hose.

- Thin and small plastic cutting board

- Two 2' lengths of paracord (ideally different colors) for practicing knot tying per *Appendix C*

Place headlamp in your pocket or around your neck BEFORE dark.

Fluff your sleeping bag; inflate pillow. I'm a big fan of down-filled bags but it's critical to keep the bag dry.

Never use a sleeping bag or inflatable mattress outside tent/shelter, especially near camp fire.

Don't overinflate your air mattress; your bodyweight will add additional firmness.

Optionally, use a sleeping bag liner to extend 3-season comfort and maintain bag cleanliness. Also functions as a blanket for summer use when no sleeping bag is needed.

Store your camp shoes, pants and hiking boots outside the tent in its vestibule.

No food or strong-scented items in or near tent. Hang all food/trash overnight using guidance in *Section 4.v (Food)*.

Affix your pack's rain cover before bedding down. You never know.

During tick season, meticulously scan your entire body daily (before dusk if possible). See *First-Aid Procedures* for tick removal guidance.

IMPORTANT (and yet another good reason to keep your tent zipped up when not in use):

Return your sleeping bag (especially if down-filled) into its stuff sack each morning to prevent it from absorbing moisture (its enemy number one), especially in summer or damp weather. No need to use the stuff sack's compression straps.

Joshua Tree National Park, CA

What to take to bed (in the tent):

- Water bottle

- In cool/cold weather, a separate 16 oz. wide-mouth plastic bottle with a tight-sealing lid marked "poison". Gents, relieve those middle-of-the-night "gotta go" urges from the comfort of your tent without even getting fully out of your sleeping bag. Talk about your weight/space-to-value item. Crazy good advice, especially for the more senior among us. Sorry, ladies.

- Small pack of tissues

- Rx / meds, lip balm

- Headlamp, earplugs

- Book, music, ear buds, journal, pencil

- Bear spray / firearm

- Knife, whistle

- See additional tips in *Winter Camping* section

Use two hands to <u>operate all zippers slowly and carefully</u>, especially tent doors, jackets and sleeping bags. Please heed this advice.

Obviously except when entering or exiting, keep your tent doors zippered shut at all times.

Use compression sacks for packing sleeping bag and clothing to maximize usable backpack capacity.

Do not skimp when buying boots, socks, sleeping bag, air mattress, tent, cookware, stove and headlamp.

Never pack glass items (save for small bottles inside First-Aid kit).

A telescoping hiking pole is recommended. Some prefer using two (more useful on open trails).

- A simple stick fashioned from a tree will suffice

- An adjustable trekking pole (having a strap through which the hand passes) is very useful on downhill trudges with a sore extremity

- Can be used to support a makeshift tarp-based shelter

- Useful for clearing cobwebs when en route in forests

Affix glow-in-the-dark tape to key items to allow quick nighttime finding using headlamp.

Protect/move fabric items away from the camp fire before bedding down (backpack, camp chair, clothing, etc.).

I repeat, never use an air mattress or sleeping bag outside of your tent/shelter.

Don't waste your money on cheap carabiners. Buy climbing-quality hardware instead. Admittedly overkill for attaching items to the outside of a backpack or rigging a campsite tarp, but the real deal will never fail and you never know when an issue/condition will arise that makes you glad you have them.

Unless your day hike is short (~four miles round trip) and is on a familiar, well-marked trail, it's wise to pack for a day hike with spending the night in mind. An unexpected injury or fast-approaching storm can derail the best laid plan. Don't be caught off guard. The few extra pounds is very cheap insurance, and could be lifesaving.

Each hiking party should divide the load and carry only one of the following:

NAVIGATION – Carry and know how to use a topographical contour map and compass (and GPS unit, if available)

FIRST-AID KIT - include First-Aid procedure flashcards, sun screen

WATER FILTER / PURIFICATION TABLETS and a collapsible 1-gallon bladder for creating a stash if water is scarce

REPAIR KIT AND TOOLS – Duct tape, Swiss army knife (w/scissors)

EMERGENCY SHELTER – one of the most important items during an emergency survival situation. For every two hikers in the party, a grommeted tarp (8' x 10') and 50' of paracord should be carried by a single person.

Every person should carry:

SUN PROTECTION – Sunglasses, hat, SPF30+ lip balm. Protect your skin and eyes against UV rays responsible for sunburns and skin cancer. Long pants and long-sleeved shirts afford best skin protection.

INSULATION – Rain coat, gloves, warm hat, warm shirt, space blanket. Be prepared for sudden changes in weather conditions. Pack extra clothing that will protect against the most extreme conditions you could encounter. If forced to hunker down overnight, create insulation between you and the heat-robbing ground using leaves, twigs, needles, moss and day pack.

LIGHT – Headlamps are preferred since they're hands-free. Conserve usage. Many offer a strobe feature for signaling/rescue. Pack extra batteries (and your whistle and hiking pole, too).

HEAT – Fire can be a heat source and an emergency signal (burn green wood/leaves to make smokiest fire). Pack waterproof matches, a lighter and some man-made, fail-proof fire starter/tinder.

WATER – Carry one-quart minimum. If hiking in hot weather, drink water often and before you feel thirsty. Prepare water before needed; do not allow yourself to become dehydrated. Before heading out on your trip, identify highly-probable en route water resources and carry the appropriate amount of water accordingly.

FOOD - Pack an extra day's supply of no-cook, easy-to-digest items having high-energy and nutritional value such as jerky, nuts, dried fruit, powdered mixes, climber's energy goo/shots and granola/power bars.

Longs Peak Keyhole- Rocky Mountain N.P., CO
(as seen from the boulder field campsite)

Gear

Choose a pack based on your child's age, size and fitness. Figure on them carrying twenty percent of their body weight.

Start their early backpacking experiences using their day pack / book bag used for school. They're already comfortable with this item anyway, providing them with a sense of security.

Don't spend a fortune on gear until your children are clearly enthused about backpacking AND are big enough to wear a real (frame) backpack.

In their early backpacking years, they'll be fine carrying a light load on their day packs, including a lightweight foam sleeping pad and an inexpensive, synthetic-filled sleeping bag with a decent comfort rating.

As for clothing, apply the same adult clothing guidance offered within *Section 2*.

Restrict your initial outings to be relatively easy and in warmer weather. Target spending one or two nights at most, hiking on established trails with mild elevation gains.

Therefore, it's not necessary to invest in hiking boots initially. Simple tennis shoes will suffice, and they'll quickly grow out of their shoes anyway. Do pack spare socks.

Load

Plan on each child carrying their own sleeping bag and pad (both lashed onto outside of day pack), clothing, snacks/light food items, headlamp and 16 ounces of water).

In general, I've found that kids love sleeping in their own (adult-less) tent. One lucky adult will likely be carrying it. Again, don't invest a fortune in some high-quality item.

Fully load their pack and take a one-mile trial hike around the neighborhood. Make adjustments accordingly.

Food

Dinners (and possibly lunch) food will likely be carried by the adults. If weight is an issue, go with freeze-dried food.

Pack simple, ready-to-eat items where possible.

To simplify things, avoid cooking with flame where possible (save for dinner, and heating water for breakfast).

Add high energy bars to their packs. Throw in some high-quality, flavored drink powders to jazz up their water routine.

Discourage kids from drinking too much near bedtime, to improve your own sleep by avoiding the "mommy I have to pee" calls while you're deep in REM land. Same goes for you.

Entertainment

- Games (with prizes)

  ▪ If near gently-running water, conduct races comprised of "boats" selected from any natural floating item

- Conduct a nature treasure hunt (see *Appendix D*). Offer prizes that provide a combination of immediate and deferred gratification:

  - Sweet treats

  - Small harmonica

  - Coupon for lightening their pack load; each good for one item to be carried for them, on one day of their choosing

  - Coupon for one backpacking gear item

  - Coupon for one field guide

Education

Review your children's science textbook and tailor the focus of backpacking topics based on what they're studying currently. Consider the woods to be their lab.

Depending upon their age, packing a small field guide in each of their packs is an item worth its weight in gold. Choose topics aligned to their individual interests. Encourage sharing.

Gently teach about things that are visible and touchable, which is more impactful especially for younger children.

Encourage your children to learn one camping and First-Aid skill each day. E.g., how to identify poison plants and how to check for (and remove) ticks.

Foster a learning environment through camp fire chats. Pose age-appropriate questions about nature to make them think about its various aspects. E.g., time (how old is ..., how long did it take for ..., etc.), symbioses and interdependencies, similarities and differences between humans and other life forms. Let them think out loud. Pull, don't push. When on a trail break or at camp next, circle back on these discussions and hone in on one or two topics that piqued their interest.

Challenge them to guess the time of moonrise/set, sunrise/set and dawn/dusk.

Learn and practice tying basic knots.

Learn about clouds and weather, and sun/moon/seasons cycles. No better time to learn about the night sky.

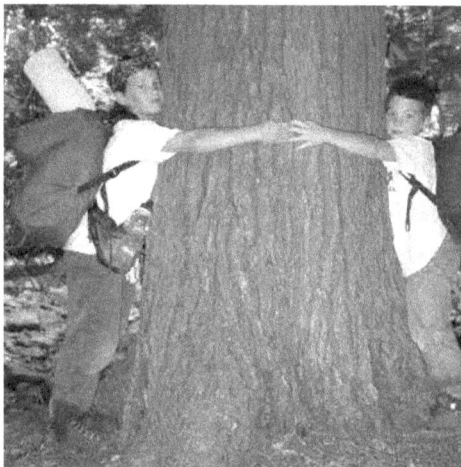

Lucky to Hug an Eastern Hemlock

Winter camping offers its own unique experience and rewards. Granted, it's not for everyone, but the right gear is everything, and makes the difference between a memorable or miserable experience.

Prior to departing, ensure that everyone in the party understands the winter-related risks (e.g., frostbite, hypothermia, snow blindness) per *Appendix B - First-Aid Procedures*. Ensure that the party understands that winter camping is no time for machismo – if someone is cold, tired, injured or hungry ... speak up!

Winter trips generally are shorter in length and duration, which compensates for the additional pack loads that winter camping requires. My advice is to do a year or more of backpacking in the other seasons before investing in the additional (and expensive) gear that winter camping requires:

- **Tent** - While you might get away using your 3-season tent for winter camping, use a four-season tent if any snow/wind is forecast. Better safe than sorry.

- **Insulated Hi-top Boots** - Size while wearing a thin liner sock (e.g., silk) and a heavy winter sock. DO NOT undersize. A snug but not tight foot movement is needed to maintain circulation and stay warm. Too loose-fitting is nearly as bad as too tight. Find your sweet spot. Don't rely on foot warmers to keep you warm. Boots having removable wool felt liners are effective and affordable. Use foot powder to help keep feet dry in cold weather.

- **Sleeping bag** - Assuming that most bags are overrated by 10 degrees, an 800-fill goose down bag rated at zero degrees (F) will reasonably keep you warm down to +10 degrees F, which is plenty cold enough to truly experience winter camping without entering the realm of the expedition-level winter camping (requiring even more expensive gear and an increased level of survival risk). Such conditions are beyond the scope of this book.

If possible, buy the longer sized sleeping bag, to allow for overnight storage of critical items in the foot of the bag per *Tips* below.

- **Other cold-weather gear**, in addition to the spring, fall and winter items listed in *Clothing* section 2.i:

    o Down-filled booties are nice to have as a camp shoe in near or below-freezing temps, providing warm and dry feet around camp, and in the sleeping bag, if needed.
    o Stuffed pillow. Avoid inflatable pillows in winter.
    o Ski goggles (or minimally, sunglasses)

Winter Camping Tips

Try winter camping (car camping or backyard) before attempting winter backpacking.

Keep dry! Do not over-sweat or over-heat. Remember that dry = warm in cool weather.

Eat high-calorie foods often. Fuel that furnace.

Exploit the cold temps and indulge in foods that would quickly perish in milder seasons. If your winter trip's weather is forecast to not exceed daytime temps in the mid-thirties (i.e., the operating temp of your fridge) then you're set to bring most any food desired. Live it up and celebrate this gift, but be prepared to keep such foods from freezing in the field.

Stay hydrated and remember that alcohol makes you colder.

No flames of any kind inside tent. Ever.

Bag these items and place them in your sleeping bag's foot box overnight: water bottle, water filter, headlamp, phone, spare batteries.

Keep water filter on body if daytime temps are below freezing.

Skip taking a water filter if snow cover and camp fire are assured,

Turn off phone to conserve battery (or minimally set to airplane mode if leaving powered on for photography purposes). Keep on person at all times.

Place your camp pad under air mattress at bedtime for insulation, especially if using a 3-season, un-insulated air mattress. In fact, it's worth considering investing in a separate air mattress designed for cold conditions. What you sleep on is as important as what you sleep in. This is another reason why it's advised to test your winter gear at home, to understand its limits. You can't afford to discover in the wild that your winter gear is inadequate.   I've been on trips with inadequately prepared folks who were forced to "sleep" by the fire. Not pretty.

Don't count on a fire to keep you warm. Be prepared to stay warm using solely your gear and knowledge. The warmth of a camp fire is merely a bonus point.

Be very conservative when planning the length and duration of a winter trip, allowing ample time for slow, yet steady, hiking and resting, and also for setting up camp and gathering firewood in daylight

Pack micro-spikes to cover icy conditions.

For safety/rescue purposes:

- Ensure that everyone understands the route (in and out), especially if hiking off trail
- Do not winter camp in groups smaller than four. This allows for two to safely seek help while the third person attends to the infirmed.

White Mountains N.F., NH

5. RETURN / UNPACK

- Dry the tent parts and sleeping bag

- Store sleeping bag and tent uncompressed, in separate bags inside mice-proof bins

- Store pillow with air mattress

- Remove insoles and dry your boots

    o Loosely stuff each boot with a rumpled newspaper page; replace paper daily for 3 days
    o Never dry boots in the sun

- Sharpen knives

- Remove batteries from headlamps and other gear

- See additional guidance in Appendix F

Appendix A - FIRST-AID KIT CONTENTS

Build your own kit using a soft-shelled, full-zippered, multi-compartment, nylon storage pouch measuring approximately 6"W x 9"L x 2-3"H.

Note: Rx covered in *Personal Items* section

ITEM	SIZE	Qty	USAGE
Dressings and Bandages			
Sterile gauze pads	4" x 4"	4	Cover wounds
Non-adherent dressings	4" x 4"	3	Abrasions and burns
Triangular bandage	36" x 36" x 52"	1	Lg. dressings, limb slings, secure a dressing
OTC Feminine hygiene pads	Medium	2	Deep wounds / bleeding
Steri-strips (sheets)	Narrow, Medium	1 ea.	Seal cut/wound (skilled use)
Butterfly bandages	Medium	4	Seal cuts/wounds
Ace wrap	N/A	1	Brace sprains, soreness
Band-aids	Assorted	8	Minor cuts & abrasions

ITEM	SIZE	Qty	USAGE
Self-adherent surgical tape	1"W x 10'L	1	Attach bandage/ dressing to skin
Cotton swabs	N/A	8	Store in small, sealable bag
Tinctures, Ointments, Antiseptics			
Antibiotic cream	2 oz.	2	Apply to small wounds / cuts pre- bandaging
Burn cream	2 oz.	2	Minor burns
Poison cream	2 oz.	2	Poison
Hydrogen peroxide	2 oz.	1	Wound cleaner
Benzoin tincture	.5 oz.	1	Makes Steri- strip stick (skilled use)
Betadyne swabs	Package	2	Wound cleaner. Antiseptic.
Cortisone cream	2 oz.	1	Itching / rash
Medicine			
Aspirin	325mg	8	Minor pain, angina
Acetaminophen (Tylenol)	325mg tablets	8	Minor aches / pains; reduce fever
Ibuprofen (Motrin)	200mg tablets	8	Non-steroidal, anti- inflammatory. Fever & mild- severe pain

114

ITEM	SIZE	Qty	USAGE
Naproxen *(Aleve)*	220mg tablets	8	Time-released. Swelling & pain relief
Alka-Seltzer Plus	Pkt. of 2	2	Cold/flu
Benadryl	25/50 mg tablets	6	Bug bites / stings, mild allergic reactions. Causes drowsiness.
Miscellaneous			
Moleskin	4" x 4"	2	Blisters
Hard candy / liquid glucose	Packet	4	Low blood sugar (hypoglycemia)
Electrolyte powder	Packet	4	Re/Dehydration
Sunscreen SPF30+	4 oz.	1	Sun protection
H_2O treatment	Tablets	8	Use when H_2O filter or fire sterilization is unavailable
Visine	2 oz.	1	Flush eye irritants
Eyeglass repair kit	Small	1	Repair eyeglasses
Splinter-Out tool	N/A	2	Remove splinters
Tick removal key	N/A	1	Keep sanitized. Store in small sealable bag

ITEM	SIZE	Qty	USAGE
Epi-pen	N/A	1	Severe allergic reactions
Scissors	Small	1	Assorted
Black *Sharpie* pen	N/A	1	Snake bite first-aid markings
First-Aid Procedures flash cards	N/A	1	Various
Earplugs	Pairs	4	Avoid campmate sleeplessness / insanity caused by loud snorers
Oral thermometer	N/A	1	Take body temp
Oxygen*	Canister	1	Breathing difficulty at high altitude
Lung inhaler*	Canister	1	Pulmonary edema (*see First-Aid Procedures*)
Metal mirror	~2"x3"	1	Rescue signaling

* Needed only for high-altitude (> 9,000') trips

116

Appendix B - FIRST-AID PROCEDURES

These procedures cover the basics and address the majority of backcountry medical conditions. It is solid information but is by no means all-encompassing. For example, it's absent instructions on how to apply stitches.

If you've obtained this book in hardcopy form then please pack it on every trip. Protect by covering the bind edge and front and back covers with clear packing tape.

It is also recommended to create separate hardcopy flashcards from *Appendix B – First-Aid Procedures* as failsafe tact, as follows:

1- Use your phone to photograph the (14) *Appendix B* flashcards and the *First Aid Report Form* (one page/photo)
2- Upload the photos to your desktop
3- Print one copy of each of the (14) flashcards and two copies of the *First Aid Report* form. Standard 8.5" x 11" paper is OK.

4- Cutout the fourteen flashcards, trimming all to a common size

5- Assemble seven two-sided flashcards. Pair (front/back) using the verbiage from the first line of each card's text, as follows:

FRONT		**BACK**
1. First Aid Response	< >	Wounds
2. Neck & Back Injuries	< >	Fractures, Dislocations...
3. Signs/Sym... Shock	< >	Burns
4. Signs...Hypothermia	< >	First-Aid ... Hypothermia
5. Heat Exhaustion	< >	First-Aid for Heat Exhaustion
6. Superficial Frostbite	< >	First-Aid for Superficial Frostbite
7. High-... Pulm. Edema	< >	Acute Mountain Sickness

6- Laminate the seven flashcards, or cover each flashcard completely with clear packing tape then trim

7- Store flashcards in zip-lock bag in First-Aid kit

8- Place a small sharpened pencil and two folded copies of the First *Aid Report Form* into a separate zip-lock bag. Do not laminate / tape. Store in First-Aid kit.

... start on next page

Swiftcurrent Pass – Glacier N. P., MT

FIRST AID RESPONSE

1. Take charge of the situation
2. Assess area. Approach the victim safely
3. Perform First-Aid
4. Protect, calm and comfort the victim
5. Check for other injuries
6. Plan what to do next
7. Carry out the plan and First-aid

- SHOCK: A critical drop in blood pressure.
- Keep tetanus vaccine / shots up-to-date to prevent future infection.
- DO NOT share any medication.

Neck and Back Injuries

- The nerve cells in the spinal cord are almost entirely incapable of healing, therefore damage may be permanent. Immobilize the victim
- Victims of spinal injury are sensitive to changes in temperature

Chest Injuries

- A serious puncture wound to the chest can kill as fast as a severed artery
- A sucking wound's sound can be heard on both inhalation and exhalation
- Victim should breathe as heavily as possible to reduce the risk of pneumonia

First Aid for Chest Puncture Wound

1. Seal the Wound by covering with sterile dressing(s)
2. Cover dressing with occlusive (airtight) dressing; Tape in place.
3. Watch closely for changes

Abdominal Injuries

- Signs of internal injury may be subtle and close attention should be paid to the signs and symptoms of shock
- Other internal injury signs include bruising, rigidity, tenderness

Wounds

- Priorities: control bleeding, prevent infection; Immobilize victim.
- To prevent infection wash hands and wound
- Close wound w/ butterfly bandage if gaping
- Puncture wounds should be left open
- Scalp wounds can be closed by tying hair together

Head Injury

- Scalp wounds bleed profusely -- easy to become overly alarmed
- Brain injuries most common cause of death in Mountaineering accidents
- Weak pulse may indicate blood loss
- Thorough head-to-toe examination is important
- Major head injury signs: changes in consciousness, skull indentations, blood or fluid draining from the ears, eye dilation, bruises behind ears or under eyes, slow pulse

Fractures, Dislocations, and Sprains

- First Aid for fractures and dislocations is splinting
- When in doubt always treat injury as a fracture
- Pay attention to victim –fracture can wait but the airways cannot.
- Injuries are potentially life-threatening and an open fracture can be missed if not stripped to bare skin.
- When the injury has affected blood flow evacuation, must be addressed ASAP. When pulse can't be found a check for capillary refill may be used   (press toe/fingernail; watch for return of color/blood to pressed area).
- Basic rule is to immobilize both adjacent joints

Basic Principles of Splinting

1. Determine the extent of the injury
2. Stop any bleeding
3. Rinse dirt off exposed bone ends, cover with sterile dressing.
4. Straighten badly angulated limbs by gentle pulling
5. Prepare a splint, size it, and pad it. Tie the splint on.
6. Observe below site for circulation/sensation. Adj. as needed.
7. Elevate the injured extremity
8. Apply cold compresses to the injury site (use snow/cold stream water if avail.)

Signs and Symptoms of Shock

Early Signs	Early Symptoms
Restlessness	Thirstiness
Face pale, gray, yellow	Nausea
Rapid pulse	Anxiety
Later Signs	**Later Symptoms**
Skin cold and damp	Lethargy and apathy
Shallow, rapid breathing	
Irregular, weak pulse	

First Aid for Shock

1. Keep airway open and clear; Control all obvious bleeding.
2. Maintain body temperature
3. Position victim to aid breathing & circulation of blood to the core
4. Avoid rough or excessive handling of the victim
5. Frequently take and record vital signs. Evacuate to med. care.

Signs and Symptoms of Mild Hypothermia

- Oral temperature down to 95 ° F (35° C)
- Complaints of cold. Shivering. Difficulty with using the hands
- Psychological withdrawal and apathy

First Aid

1. End exposure—get the victim out of cold and wet
2. Replace wet clothing with dry or add insulation
3. Place the victim in a warm environment (body-to-body if needed)
4. Offer warm liquids/foods if victim is fully conscious & able to swallow easily

Signs and Symptoms of Moderate or Severe Hypothermia

- Oral temperatures lower than 95 ° F (35 ° C)
- Lethargy, mental confusion, refusal to recognize problem
- Uncontrollable shivering; Slurred speech; Stumbling.

More Severe Signs:

- Unresponsiveness; Decreased pulse and respiration.
- Cessation of shivering; Physical *collapse* *… more info on back …*

BURNS

Small fragments of adhered cloth should **not** be removed from wound

Minor – Immerse burn area in cold water until pain subsides. Air dry; protect blisters by covering with a <u>dry</u> sterile dressing.
Major - Plunge burn area ASAP in cold water <u>for at least 10 minutes.</u> Once the "fire" is out, wash burned area. Remove rings, jewelry. Air dry; then apply a <u>dry</u>, sterile dressing. No ointment! Wrap in an occlusive dressing. Elevate a burned extremity. Assess victim thoroughly. Evacuate.

SNOW BLINDNESS

- Victim has bloodshot, tearing eyes
- Prevention/care: place tape over the (sun)glasses lenses leaving a horizontal slit. - Pain relief: cool wet compress, aspirin. No anesthetic ointments (e.g., *Lidacaine*) or rubbing!

First Aid for Moderate or Severe Hypothermia

First Aid if **Victim Will Be Evacuated Promptly**:
- End exposure—cover victim rather than walking victim to shelter
- Treat victim gently—clothing may have to be cut to prevent unnecessary movement
- DO NOT allow victim to move
- Check for other injury including frostbite (see other page)

Further First Aid if **No Prompt Evacuation**:
- Re-warming victim should focus on delivering warmth to the head, neck, armpits, and groin areas. Warmth may be delivered by application of warm water bottles, warmed blankets, or another body.
- Offer warm food or liquid only when the victim is fully conscious and has no difficulty swallowing

... DIAGNOSIS AIDS ON OTHER SIDE ...

Heat Exhaustion

Signs	Symptoms
Pale skin color	Nausea
Profuse sweating	Weakness
Skin Temperature normal or cool	Dizziness
Oral temperature normal or high	Thirst
	Headache

Heat Stroke

Signs	Symptoms
Irrational, confused, combative	Weakness
Pale, damp, cool skin/red, hot dry skin	Irritability
Oral temperature > 105 º F	Dizziness, headache

... TREATMENT OPTIONS ON OTHER SIDE ...

Superficial Frostbite

Signs	Symptoms
Small patches of white/waxy skin	Pain may be felt early
Patches are hard to the touch, underlying soft tissues	Area may feel intensely cold / numb

Deep Frostbite

Signs	Symptoms
Skin is white and may be waxy to the touch	Pain may be felt as the part freezes
Skin hard to touch, underlying tissues are **solid**	Part may become numb / senseless
Joint movement absent or restricted	Part will be very painful thawing
Area may be as small as part of a finger or whole limb	

... TREATMENT OPTIONS ON OTHER SIDE ...

First Aid for Heat Exhaustion

- Place victim in a cool, shady environment
- Give victim water in sips (electrolyte solutions may be used)
- Activity should not be resumed until the signs and symptoms are completely gone. Observe the victim for recurrence of heat exhaustion.

First Aid for Heat Stroke

DECREASE BODY TEMPERATURE:

- Remove or loosen clothing
- Place victim in cool, shady environment
- Cool the victim with cool cloths or cool water applied to head, neck, armpits and groin. Vigorous fanning helps.

If victim is conscious, give water in sips

Victim must be carried out and needs hospitalization

... DIAGNOSIS AIDS ON OTHER SIDE ...

First Aid for Superficial Frostbite

- Place a warm body part next to the frozen area, applying firm steady pressure
- **DO NOT RUB** the area
- Protect the area from further freezing

First Aid for Deep Frostbite

1. KEEP THE FROZEN PART FROZEN
2. Prevent further injury: AVOID rubbing and further freezing of unaffected tissue
3. If the part has thawed, the part should NOT be allowed to refreeze or bear weight. A victim with thawed feet should be carried out.
4. Give victim plenty of fluids
5. Evacuate as soon as possible

... DIAGNOSIS AIDS ON OTHER SIDE ...

High Altitude Pulmonary Edema

Signs	Symptoms
A dry cough at first, later producing watery sputum (may become pink)	Headache and/or dizziness
Gurgling sounds	Nausea, no appetite
Very rapid pulse	Difficulty breathing
Victim becomes incoherent, may have hallucinations	Increasing anxiety
In last stage, victim drops into to coma, death in 6-12 hours	Weakness, fatigue

First Aid for High Altitude Pulmonary Edema

- Descend, descend, descend to a lower altitude at the first indication of pulmonary edema. If descent is not possible, victim must be carefully monitored for breathing difficulties, particularly at night
- Assist breathing as necessary (w/lung inhaler or acetazolamide aka., *Diamox*, Rx taken orally; diuretic effect)

Acute Mountain Sickness

Signs	Symptoms
Difficulty with sleep	Mild-to-severe headache
Unusual breathing patterns, more obvious @ night & during sleep	Weakness and dull muscle pain
Fast, bounding pulse at rest	Lack of appetite, nausea
Vomiting, decreased/dark urine	Dizziness
Puffiness in hands and face	Shortness of breath

First Aid for Acute Mountain Sickness

- Make conscious effort to breathe deeply and regularly, or thorough pursed lips. If dizziness or nausea develops, stop conscious breathing effort.
- Slow down the pace of travel, learn/use the "rest step" . Increase the amount of fluids drunk. At high altitude, dehydration is a threat.
- Aspirin for minor headache.   Rest if symptoms make travel difficult.
- If symptoms are beyond a reasonable level of discomfort, descend

FIRST-AID REPORT		
CHECK	FINDINGS	FIRST-AID GIVEN
Airway (A) Breathing (B) Circulation (C)	A: B: C:	
Initial Rapid Check Chest wounds, Severe bleeding		
Hurts where? Happened How?		
Pulse (P) and Respiration (R)	P: R:	
HEAD		
NECK		
CHEST		
ABDOMEN		
PELVIS		
EXTREMETIES		
BACK		
SKIN Color (C)	C:	
SKIN Temp (T)	T:	
SKIN Moistness (M)	M:	
Medical ID Tag? Allergies?		
Victim's Name		
Form Completed By / Date		

Additional First-Aid Procedures

Ticks

There are a variety of parasites, bacteria and viruses borne by deer ticks. Among the more common is Lyme's disease, caused by the bacteria *Borrelia burgdorfer*. The tick should be carefully removed as soon as possible. The longer an infected tick remains attached to a person or animal, the higher the likelihood of disease transmission. If available, remove using the tick key tool per below; else use fine-point tweezers to grip the mouthparts of the tick as close to your skin as possible. The tick should not be squeezed or twisted, but pulled straight outward with steady, gentle pressure. You should not apply kerosene, petroleum jelly, nail polish, or a hot match tip to remove the tick. These measures are not effective and may result in injury. Make note of the date and note where on the body the tick was removed. Circle the area using Sharpie. You may want to save the tick for identification. Your physician may choose to treat you following a deer tick bite. Notify your health care provider if you have been bitten by a deer tick or if you develop a rash or other signs of illness following a tick bite.

Removal using tick key: place the large opening of key around the tick, with the narrow end pointing toward the tick's head. Slide key flush against skin, slowly pulling (do not lift key) toward the rear of the tick's body to catch its head and dislodge tick

entirely from your skin. Works on pets, too. Treat area with liquid antiseptic then apply antibiotic cream and cover with band-aid. Sanitize tick key after each use. Store in First-Aid kit in a clean, re-sealable bag.

Deer ticks are the smallest tick in North America. Adults grow to about the size of a sesame seed, yet you can feel them moving on your skin. They are distinctly reddish and have a solid black dorsal (back) shield with long, thin mouth parts.

These instructions pertain to treating bites from vipers (e.g., rattlesnake, copperhead, cottonmouth / water moccasin and sidewinder). Copperhead bites are more common in North America but rattlesnake bites are more damaging. The odor emitted by the Eastern Timber Rattler has been described as distinctly musky, or the smell of *Dorito* chips. Copperheads smell of cucumbers.

If you will be hiking in a part of the world having elapid snakes whose venom contains deadly neurotoxins (e.g., mambas, coral, all Australian snakes) then do your research to learn their distinct treatment guidance.

Ultimately you're going to need anti-venom as it's the only definitive treatment for an envenomation (poisoning by venom). The treatment guidance below is designed to help get you to civilization and be treated.

Perform the following steps in the event of a bite in the backcountry from any species of venomous snake:

- DO NOT USE A TOURNIQUET

- DO NOT CUT AND SUCK

- DON'T USE STUN GUNS (TASER). NO SCIENTIFICALLY-BASED STUDIES COMFIRM EFFICACY. BENEFITS ARE ANECDOTAL.

- DO NOT APPLY A VENOM EXTRACTOR OR USE "SNAKEBITE KITS"

- DO NOT FOLLOW ANY STRANGE RECOMMENDATIONS YOU MAY RECEIVE

- NO FIRST AID IS OFTEN LESS HARMFUL THAN BAD FIRST AID WHEN IT COMES TO SNAKEBITES

1) **Carefully walk backwards and find a safe space to sit down nearby** before the venom drops your blood pressure and you pass out and hit your head. Many snake venoms disrupt blood clotting and the last thing you want is to cause internal bleeding on top of your snakebite complications.

2) **Remove any rings, watches, bracelets, and anything else that could become a tourniquet if your limb swells.** These items can be very difficult or impossible to remove once swelling has occurred, so exercise some foresight and remove them right away.

3) **Circle the site of the bite with a sharpie and write the time next to it. Mark the edge of the swelling and pain, make a list of your symptoms, and repeat every 30 minutes or so.** Always record the time next to each mark. The vast majority of snakebites can be diagnosed and treated by your symptoms and severity of the envenomation without requiring a positive identification of the species responsible. That's why this is so important!

4) **If you begin to experience signs of anaphylaxis** (swelling of face, mouth, or throat; hives; difficulty breathing, etc) **use an epinephrine auto-injector** (Epi-Pen or generic) if you have one.

5) If you have cell phone reception call 911*****, tell them where you are, when you were

bitten, and the list of current symptoms you just wrote down.

If you aren't in the U.S, look up the local emergency services number (the 911 equivalent). Add to your phone before heading out.

6) If you don't have signal/reception, plot the safest and most expedient path to find a signal or reach a vehicle (whatever is safer/faster) and then start hiking out.

Time is tissue is the snakebite treatment adage, and it may be better to walk yourself out in an hour than to sit and wait for five hours until a helicopter arrives. **The idea that one should do everything possible to avoid speeding up circulation of venom is bad advice.** You are already terrified from being bitten by a snake so your heart rate and blood pressure are already sky high. Most snakes bites in remote places result in having to hike out to reach the hospital. Figure out the fastest, safest route to find help and then make it happen.

If you can get a picture of the snake on your phone without putting yourself at risk, it will be useful, but it is not necessary by any means because snake envenomations can be diagnosed and treated by your symptoms. That's why it is so important to chart the progression of swelling and records the symptoms as they develop!

To splint, or not to splint? There are to-date no compelling studies showing any benefit. Extreme positioning (immobilizing the limb and keeping it either way above or way below the heart) does not appear to be helpful and may even increase the odds of developing a dangerous *compartment syndrome* (occurs when the pressure within a compartment increases, restricting the blood flow to the area and potentially damaging the muscles and nearby nerves. It usually occurs in the legs, feet, arms or hands, but can occur wherever there's an enclosed compartment inside the body). At best, *immobilize the limb with a sling or swath in a relatively neutral position of comfort that reduces pain.*

Pain relievers: Avoid taking any sort of NSAID analgesics for pain control after the bite, e.g., aspirin, ibuprofen (*Motrin*), *Aleve*. These medications interfere with normal blood clotting, and when combined with the nasty effects many snake venoms have on blood vessels and blood clotting, it can lead to severe internal bleeding.

Do not use ice or snow for snakebites! Coldness causes the smaller blood vessels to constrict and when combined with viper venoms it can produce dramatic tissue damage. It's better to let the swelling happen and focus on getting to a hospital.

If the threat of being bitten by a poisonous snake in the U.S.A. is intolerable, then limit your hiking to Alaska, Hawaii and Maine, where no poisonous snakes exist.

Credit: www.snakebitefoundation.org

Pacific Coast, Mendocino Co., CA

**17 mi. Day Hike Across Continental Divide
Rocky Mountain N.P., CO**

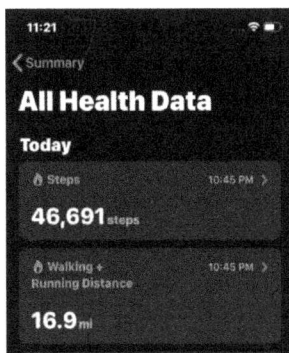

Best.

Day
hike.

Ever.

The ABC's of Cardio-Pulmonary Resuscitation are to restore (in the following order) **Airway, Breathing, and Circulation**

1. If possible, call 911

2. Lay the person on their back and open their Airway by tilting head slightly back (chin up), clearing any obstructions if applicable.

3. Check for Breathing. If they're not breathing, start CPR using the latest Circulation (resuscitation) guidance offered by the American Heart Association.

4. Resuscitation best practices change over time. Rather than offer outdated info herein, better guidance is to re-visit these guidelines annually and adjust your knowledge and methods accordingly.

How to Wrap an ACE Bandage

When you twist or sprain your ankle, putting compression on the injured area can help reduce swelling and pain. The easiest way to do this is to wrap your ankle with an ACE bandage. When wrapping, it's important to position it correctly, making sure it's not too tight and kept on for long enough to help your ankle heal. Proper wrapping can help a mildly injured ankle heal quicker and more effectively while also making the recovery period more comfortable.

1. **Roll up the ACE bandage.** If your bandage does not come in a tight roll, take the time to roll it up. Having the bandage in a roll rather than loose will make applying it easier and quicker in the long run. If your bandage comes with Velcro at one end, start rolling up from that end. You want the Velcro to end up on the end of the bandage after wrapping.

2. **Position your foot so it's at a 90-degree angle from your ankle.** Keep it at this angle during the whole process of wrapping so that the bandage doesn't slip or move accidentally. Wrapping your foot in this position will be best for circulation and comfort. Once the ankle is wrapped, the foot will be able to move a bit, so don't worry that your foot will be kept at an uncomfortable angle.

3. **Begin wrapping the bandage around the ball of your foot.** Place the end of

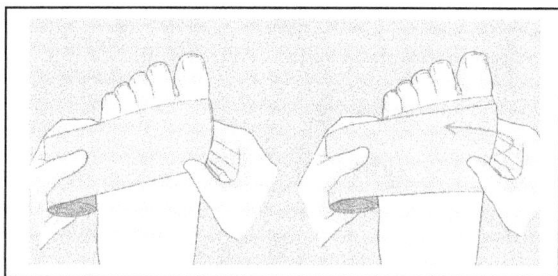

the bandage on the top of your foot next to the toes. Hold the end with one hand while you wrap the bandage down bandage is back around the top of the foot, you can tug it a little to keep it taut and to keep the end in place.

4. **Continue wrapping to the back of the arch of your foot.** It typically takes about 3 or 4 wraps to cover this area. This area gets a lot of

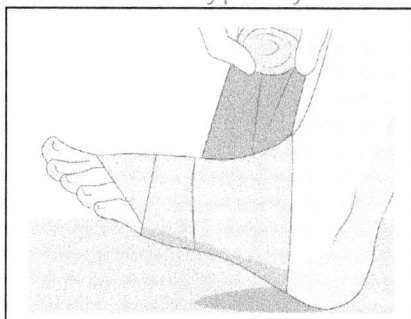

movement when you walk or put pressure on your foot, so be sure to wrap it completely. If you don't cover an area on the first pass, feel free to wrap back and forth a few times until you can no longer see any skin.

5. **Transition from your foot to your ankle.** Start moving your wraps from the back of the arch, over the heel, and to the bottom of the Achilles tendon. Go back and forth over this area a couple of times to help secure the bandage in this area. It's hard to keep the bandage from slipping off the heel. It typically likes to move up or down. This is actually OK to

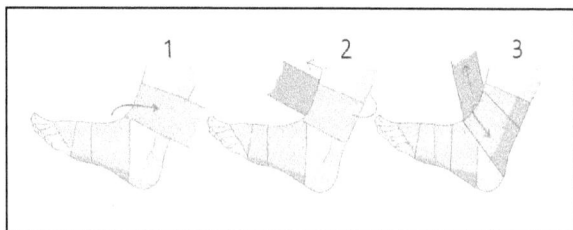

some extent, as a bit of exposed skin at the back of the heel won't prevent the bandage from giving stability and proper compression.

6. **Keep wrapping up past the ankle bone.** You want the wrap to end about 3 inches (7.6 cm) above your ankle bone if your injury is right at the ankle. Do a couple of wraps right at the top to anchor the ACE bandage. This will ensure that the bandage keeps light pressure on the injured area and stays in place.

It may take a couple tries to get your wrap to end in

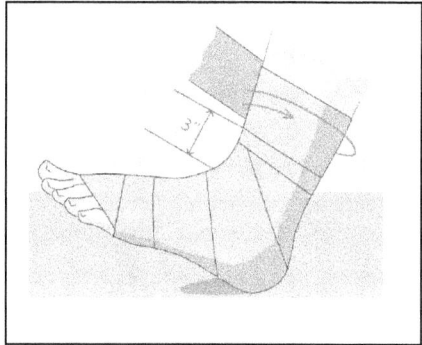

the right spot. How many turns you do over the foot and ankle depends on how long your ACE bandage is and how tightly you wrap. Double-check that you aren't wrapping it too tightly. You may need to adjust the wrap to loosen or tighten it, depending on how much compression feels comfortable.

142

7. **Overlap the layers halfway across each other.** As you work your way around your foot and ankle, make sure that the elastic overlaps the last layer you made. This will help ensure that there is the right amount of compression applied to your injury and that the bandage stays in place. The only area of skin that you should intentionally keep exposed is the toes. However, it's fine if some of the heel becomes exposed due to movement at the ankle.

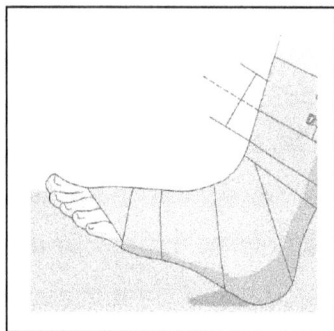

When you're done wrapping the ACE bandage, **secure the end** to the previous layer with either the **Velcro** at the end of the bandage or **clips**, whichever your bandage came with.

8. **Wrap the bandage so that it's tight but not constricting.** An elastic bandage should

be wrapped tight enough to put a small amount of compression on the ankle, but it shouldn't cause numbness, tingling, or additional pain. If you experience any of these things, loosen the bandaging you have done and continue with a looser wrap. The bandage can get overly tight over time if your injury causes swelling. If you start to feel tingling or numbness, take off the bandage and re-wrap the area.

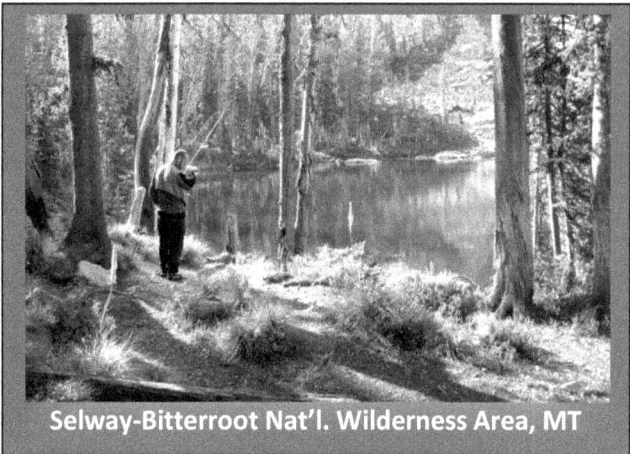

Selway-Bitterroot Nat'l. Wilderness Area, MT

Appendix C - ESSENTIAL KNOTS

While there are many hundreds of different knots, we'll focus on a small handful taken from the four primary knot categories shown below that serve the backpacking world well.

> ➤ Pack two ropes for practicing in camp, each 2'L and 1/8" thick and ideally different colors. Paracord will suffice.

1. **Loop Knots** (make a loop in a rope)

Bowline – form a secure loop at rope end

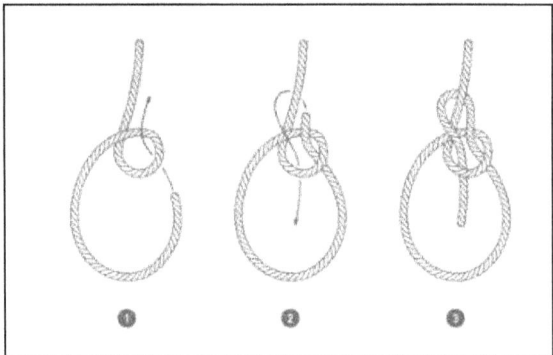

Alpine Butterfly – form secure loop in middle of a rope (create additional guy line tie-off points)

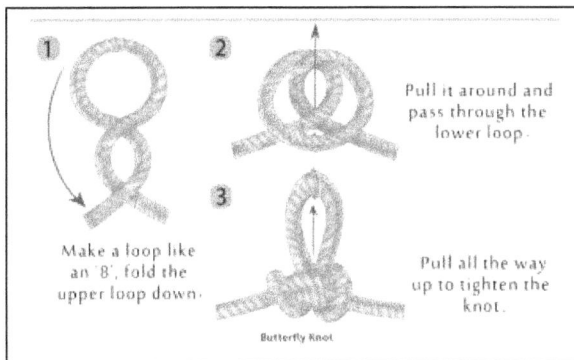

1. Make a loop like an '8', fold the upper loop down.

2. Pull it around and pass through the lower loop.

3. Pull all the way up to tighten the knot.

Butterfly Knot

2. **Bend Knots** (rope-to-rope knots)

Fisherman's – tie two ropes together

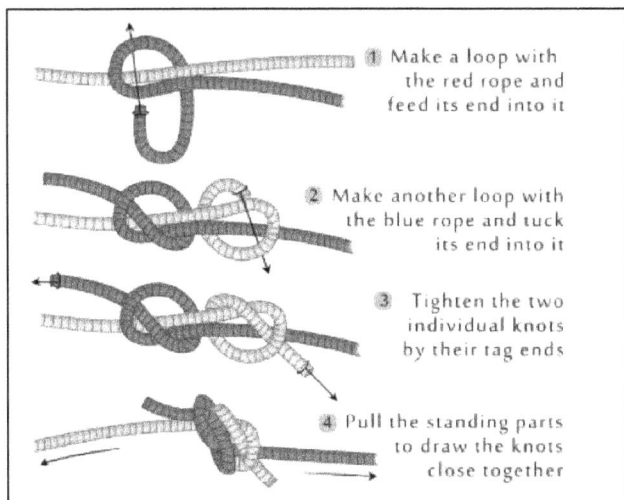

1. Make a loop with the red rope and feed its end into it

2. Make another loop with the blue rope and tuck its end into it

3. Tighten the two individual knots by their tag ends

4. Pull the standing parts to draw the knots close together

146

3. **Hitch Knots** (rope-to-object)

Clove hitch – tie rope to a post (pet, horse)

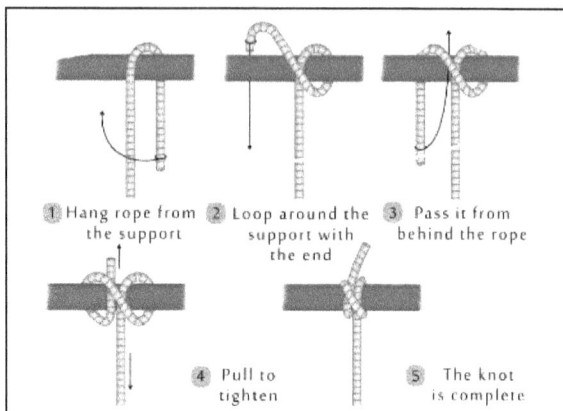

1. Hang rope from the support
2. Loop around the support with the end
3. Pass it from behind the rope
4. Pull to tighten
5. The knot is complete

Constrictor hitch – tie up bundles of items

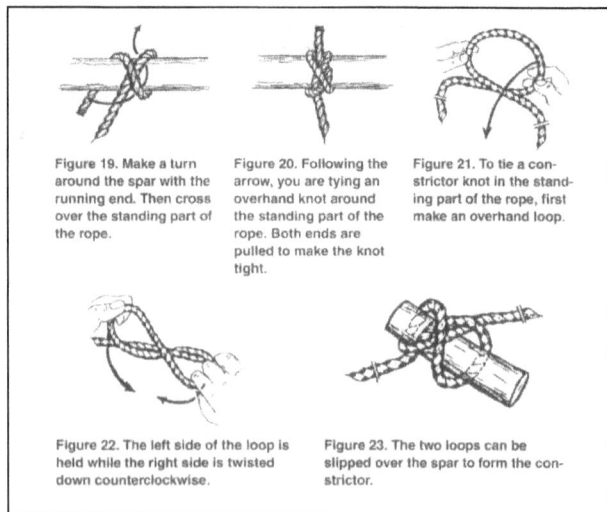

Figure 19. Make a turn around the spar with the running end. Then cross over the standing part of the rope.

Figure 20. Following the arrow, you are tying an overhand knot around the standing part of the rope. Both ends are pulled to make the knot tight.

Figure 21. To tie a constrictor knot in the standing part of the rope, first make an overhand loop.

Figure 22. The left side of the loop is held while the right side is twisted down counterclockwise.

Figure 23. The two loops can be slipped over the spar to form the constrictor.

Knute hitch – attach an object to a lanyard (knife, whistle)

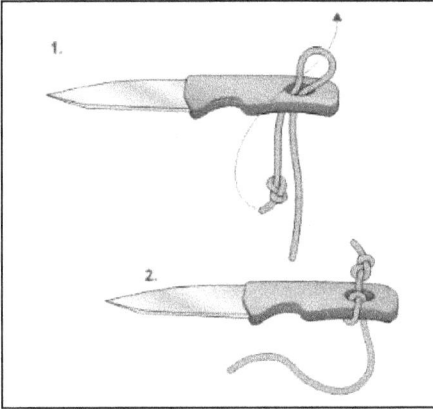

Tautline hitch – create adjustable-length line (secured around a tent stake / tree trunk/limb)

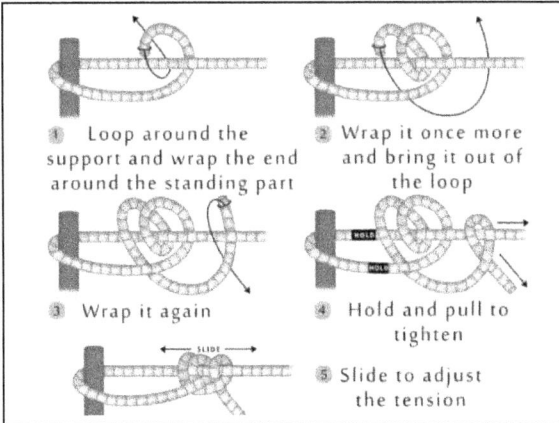

1. Loop around the support and wrap the end around the standing part

2. Wrap it once more and bring it out of the loop

3. Wrap it again

4. Hold and pull to tighten

5. Slide to adjust the tension

4. **Binding Knots** - Grip, wrap objects. Usually made with both ends of the same line. E.g., tie shoelaces, secure top of open bag.

Better Bow — tie those slippery hiking boot laces more securely

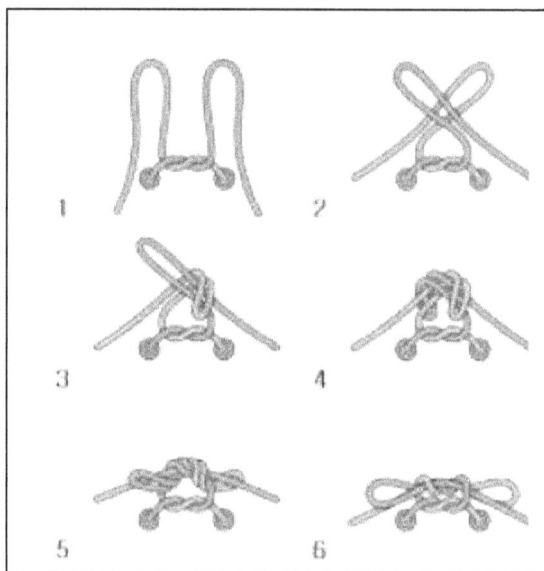

Strangle – tie up ends of bundles/sacks/bags

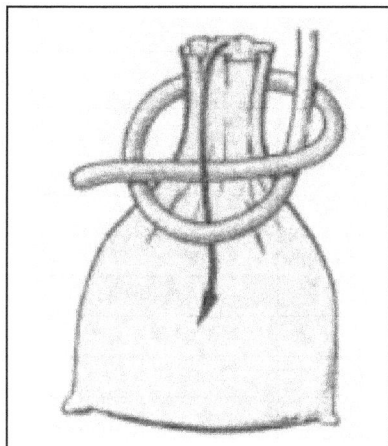

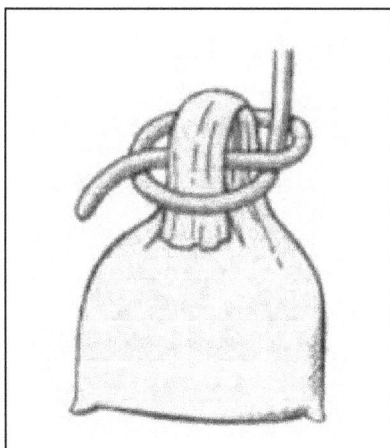

Appendix D - KIDS NATURE CHALLENGE

Name / Date:		
Identify/Gather	**Discovery / Result**	**Pts.**
Bird #1		1
Bird #2		1
Bird Feather 1		2
Bird Feather 2		2
Bird Song #1		3
Bird Song #2		3
Fern		1
Tree		1
Tree Leaf #1		1
Tree Leaf #2		1
Crawling insect photo		3
Amphibian		3
Eggshell		3
Whole egg photo		5
Nest photo		3
Fungi #1		1
Fungi #2		1
Antler		3
Horn		3
Quartz		1
Nut		1
Seed		1

Name / Date:		
ID Night Sky Object #1		2
ID Night Sky Object #2		2
ID Night Sky Object #3		2
ID Nettles		1
ID Jewelweed		1
ID Poison Ivy		1
Animal Poop photo		3
Bird Poop photo		3
Spider/Web photo		2
Flying insect photo		2
Algae photo		1
Lichen photo		1
Tie Knot x		4
Tie Knot y		4
	SCORE:	

Appendix E - PACKING CHECKLIST

First-Aid / Hygiene / Safety
(refer to section 1.i)

☐ First-Aid kit (w/laminated *Appendix B - First-Aid Procedures* cards)

☐ Bear spray and/or gun

☐ Survival knife

☐ Small Swiss Army (pocket) knife

☐ Whistle

☐ Metal trowel

☐ Wet wipes

☐ Compressed (expandable) towlettes

☐ Hand sanitizer

☐ Two 1-gallon *Zip-lock* bags (you'll find a use for them)

☐ Communications capability

☐ Map & compass

☐ Bug spray/cream (avoid DEET. Seek picaridin products)

Footwear / Clothing (refer to sections 2.i, 2.ii)

☐ Hiking boots (and insoles, if applicable)

☐ Camp shoes (stored in plastic bag)

☐ Spare socks

☐ Clothing (packed into compression sack)

☐ Hat(s)

☐ Raincoat

☐ Face net for bugs (as conditions warrant)

☐ Pocket poncho (if raincoat not packed)

☐ Gaitors (optional)

Fire / Water (refer to sections 4.iii, 4.iv)

☐ 1 gal. collapsible water transport vessel

☐ Water filter (and filter cleaner device, especially longer trips)

☐ 32 oz. water bottle (freeze half-full before topping off and packing)

☐ Backup tinder (stored in waterproof bag)

☐ Handsaw

Luxury: Backpack hydration bladder (w/ inline filter); hatchet

Food / Cooking (refer to sec. 4.vii and 4.viii)

☐ Nesting cookware set (and storage bag)

☐ Cooking and eating wares

☐ Pot lifter; small multi-purpose tool

☐ Fire glove

☐ Biodegradable liquid soap (2 oz.)

☐ 30' paracord for hanging food/trash overnight

☐ Cups (metal, double-insulated w/lid; wide-mouth, plastic w/handle)

☐ Collapsible fire grate (N/A if cooking solely by stove)

☐ Campsite trash bags (small, 2)

☐ Food (stored in stuff sack)

☐ Spices/seasonings

☐ Grapeseed oil (if needed), double-sealed

Luxury:

☐ Collapsible table

☐ Cutting board

☐ Cook stove and fuel

☐ Charcoal

☐ Bear-proof food storage canister

Shelter / Sleeping / Comfort

(refer to sections 4.ii, 4.ix)

☐ Tent, ground cloth, repair kit

☐ Sleeping bag (packed in waterproof compression sack)

☐ Pillow (stored w/sleeping bag)

☐ Air mattress

☐ Hiking pole(s)

☐ Backpack rain cover

<u>Luxury</u>:

☐ Chair

☐ Ground pad

☐ Tarp, 50' paracord

☐ Hammock (w/rope/webbing/hooks for mounting)

Personal Items (refer to section 4.vii)

☐ Headlamp w/fresh batteries (spares of both for longer trips)

☐ Toiletries

   ○ Toothbrush/paste, floss

   ○ Rx, OTC meds not stocked in First-Aid kit

   ○ Expandable towlettes (TP, etc.)

   ○ Spare contacts/saline, if applicable

   ○ Small pack tissues

☐ Feminine hygiene products (in sealable bags)

☐ Small hand towel

☐ Cotton bandana

☐ Extremities brace/support

☐ Sunglasses

☐ Eyeglass lanyard; tiny eyeglass repair kit

☐ Repair kit: 3' piece of 1/2"W *Velcro* tape rolled tight and attached to carabiner on pack. 2' roll of duct/tenacious tape for tent/fly repairs. 2 large safety pins.   Lg. sewing needle. Assorted zip-tie sizes.

Luxury Personal Items:

☐ Electronics (ear buds/music library/small Bluetooth speaker, backup battery, solar charger, cables)

☐ Reading material, card deck

☐ Prizes / treats for kids games

☐ Adult beverages

☐ Hand warmers

☐ Solar shower

☐ Journal, pen/pencil

☐ Empty 16 oz. wide-mouth plastic bottle (men only)

☐ 2 small ropes for practicing knot tying (ideally different colors)

After Each Trip

- Apply hot wax to boot leather (e.g., *Sno-Seal* brand)

- Backflush / clean water filter; replenish First-Aid kit / form

- Place your <u>dry</u> sleeping bag uncompressed in a large, mesh storage bag. Store in a plastic storage bin with a mouse-proof lid. Ditto for your tent.

Annually

- Fully assemble your tent outside then spray a light coat of silicone waterproofing onto its rain fly. Should not see pooling. Recommend *Kiwi Camp Dry* product. Allow to dry at least an hour then apply a light second coat.

- Allow tent fly to dry then disassemble tent. Set rain fly aside. Flip tent over to expose only its floor's underside. Tuck any non-floor material in under the floor. Spray floor lightly with silicone (should not see pooling). Allow to dry at least an hour then apply a light second coat.

- Spray silicone on tops of camp shoes / booties. Think of this as furniture *Scotchguard* for your footwear.

- Apply liquid silicone to all zippers

- Apply seam seal to tent floor seams and tent rain fly seams (both sides). This is separate from (and supplemental to) spraying silicone per above.

- Replace expired First-Aid kit items

- Replace expired bear pepper spray

- Review latest First-Aid guidance at large; update/replenish *Appendix B. First-Aid Procedures* accordingly. Review latest Amer. Red Cross CPR guidance; update accordingly.

- Carefully inspect all gear (inside and outside) for frayed or loose fibers/threads, carefully cauterizing any found by quickly passing the flame of a lighter near (but not directly on) the material.

  - Does not work (do not try) on non-synthetic materials (e.g., cotton, wool, silk)

  - Recommended especially for zipper threads and other seams

  - Use also on freshly-cut synthetic rope ends

  - Be extremely careful performing on tents (seams only) and down-filled items

  - Don't attempt on torn tent/tarp fabric. Instead, repair the torn area by placing tape on both sides of fabric.

  - Never pull a loose thread. Singe it instead, or tie off then snip if non-synthetic material.

Appendix G - LEAVE NO TRACE PRINCIPLES

1. Plan and Prepare
2. Travel & Camp on Durable Surfaces
3. Dispose of Waste Properly
4. Leave What You Find
5. Minimize Camp Fire Impacts
6. Respect Wildlife
7. Be Considerate of Others

Explore principles in detail at www.int.org

FIELD NOTES

FIELD NOTES

FIELD NOTES

FIELD NOTES

FIELD NOTES

About The Author

It's almost unfathomable that I've been backpacking for fifty years. That's a lot of wear on these original knees. I'm extremely fortunate to have backpacked (injury-free!) in a wide variety of terrains and four-season conditions across the continental US, including national parks, federal wilderness areas, seashores, and national and state forests. The majority of my experiences were of the primitive backcountry type, with some trail hiking, a fair dose of bushwhacking and avoiding fixed campsites if possible. No matter, the *Leave No Trace* principles were practiced to the greatest possible extent, and will always remain paramount.

I wish I had kept a journal of the places backpacked, and their accompanying trail mates. While I do possess some photos, it's mostly just wonderful memories that I'll never forget. With any luck, I have many miles to go.

On a recent trip (2022) into the splendor of mid-Appalachian autumnal foliage, where the majority of my backpacking occurred, it dawned on me that surely my experience and lessons learned could help others. And so became the genesis of this humble offering. May it benefit you, and may your trips be many and your body strong.

Acknowledgements

Firstly, thank YOU for buying this book, and for posting a positive rating! Writing it has been a true labor of love, and I hope that it benefits you greatly.

It's hard to know where to begin thanking the countless kindred souls who have enriched and taught me so much over the years.

My children, Erica and Ron, whose boundless juvenile joy exuded on many trips from an early age created so many fond memories, and provided the basis for the *Backpacking With Children* chapter. Especially fond memories were spawned by our time spent together (as adults) in Glacier N.P., MT (backpacking to Granite Park chalet on the Highline trail), Yellowstone N.P., WY, the Magruder Corridor (Nez Perce) trail, MT, and (butt sledding in) Goat Rocks wilderness in Gifford Pinchot N.F., WA.

My brother, Matt, for sharing so many trips, and providing countless and delectable fresh-caught trout and venison tenderloin dinners, expertly cooked over a camp fire.

My brothers, Todd and John, for sharing many fond trips in the forest and at ocean's edge, and brother Joe, for always being there in spirit.

My sister, Maria, and her husband, Brian, for providing many immensely important shuttles. Not to mention the cold beers and delectable home-baked goods awaiting us at trip's end.

My many wonderful nephews and nieces, who allowed their "old uncle Mark" to grace them on their inaugural trip (and many since) and, in recent years, to accompany them with their progeny, too!

My sorely-missed Montanan friend and backpacking soul mate, Loren Spencer, from whom I've learned more about backpacking than anyone. My memories of our magical trips into Montana's Selway-Bitterroot wilderness will never be forgotten. Nor will our winter camping (got lost and humbled) in the Dolly Sods, WV wilderness, full moon backpacking to Old Rag Mtn. (sampled dried rabbit terds – not recommended) in

Shenandoah N.P., VA, and numerous trips in George Washington N.F., VA, and Monongahela N.F., WV.

My dear D.C. friend, Eric Nothman, who turned me on to the marvels of the American west many moons ago, and taught me to respect a 2-mile portage and the mosquitoes of the Boundary Waters Canoe Area (BWCA), MN wilderness.

My beloved friend, Pastor Laura Hollister, who so graciously shared some beautiful places in America's northwest, especially the amazing Yellowstone N.P., WY experiences involving a moonlit herd of buffalo that sauntered single-file so near our tent that we could hear them "talking". Not to mention the eerie howling of the pack of wolves later that same night that, according to a park ranger, had prematurely escaped their acclimation pen only months before our arrival. How lucky were we to hear the original pack whose progeny now populates the Yellowstone ecosystem!

My dear, simpatico friends, Amy and Stephen Owens, who have converted me to an avid lover of Colorado's Rocky Mountains, and have taken me on many memorable hikes and backpacking trips in Rocky Mountain N.P., CO, including an unforgettable ascent of Longs Peak (with an overnighter in the Boulder Field), and a 17-mile, one-day hike from the east side of R.M.N.P, across the continental divide to its west side. Both were bucket list events and, at my age, both are likely to be of the one-and-done variety.

I could probably go on forever, but I'll end with a heartfelt THANK YOU to my lovely wife, Rhonda ... for tolerating me while writing this book, for opening her heart and feet to the outdoor world, for accompanying me on so many hikes and backpacking trips, and for shuttling me and others to and fro the trips that she couldn't join. Her domesticating presence has taught me so much about improving the creature comforts of backpacking, plus she's a killer cook and keeps a homey and clean campsite. You rock, my dear!